il Cenacolo

Guide to the Refectory
and Church of Santa Maria
delle Grazie

il Cenacolo

Pietro C. Marani
Roberto Cecchi
Germano Mulazzani

Guide to the Refectory
and Church of Santa Maria
delle Grazie

Electa

Cover illustration
Santa Maria delle Grazie,
detail of the vaults of the chapels

Translation by Margaret Kunzle
and Felicity Lutz for Scriptum, Rome

This volume was published by Electa, Milan
Elemond Editori Associati

Map of Santa Maria delle Grazie and Its Refectory

Key

I   Large Cloister
II Refectory with the *Last Supper*
III Church of Santa Maria delle Grazie
IV Bramantesque apse and choir
V   Lady Chapel
VI New Sacristy
VII Small Cloister
VIII Old Sacristy
IX Cloister of the Prior

1 Leonardo, *Last Supper*
2 Donato Montorfano, *Crucifixion*
3 Chapel of Saint Catherine
4 Frescoes by Gaudenzio Ferrari
5 Wooden choir
6 Vault with Leonardesque "knots"
7 Frescoes in the Lady Chapel

Services

A *reception and ticket office*
B *toilets*
C *bookshop*

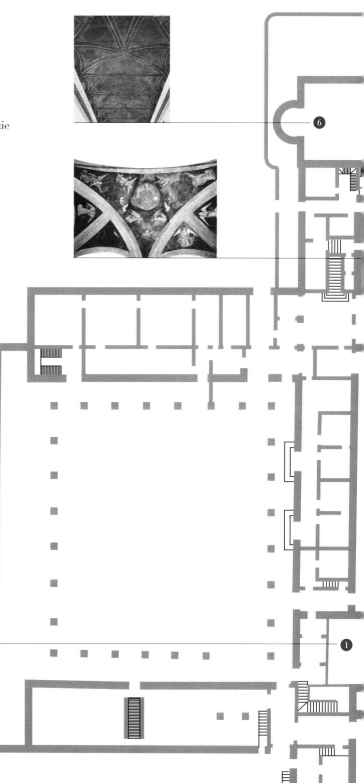

Contents

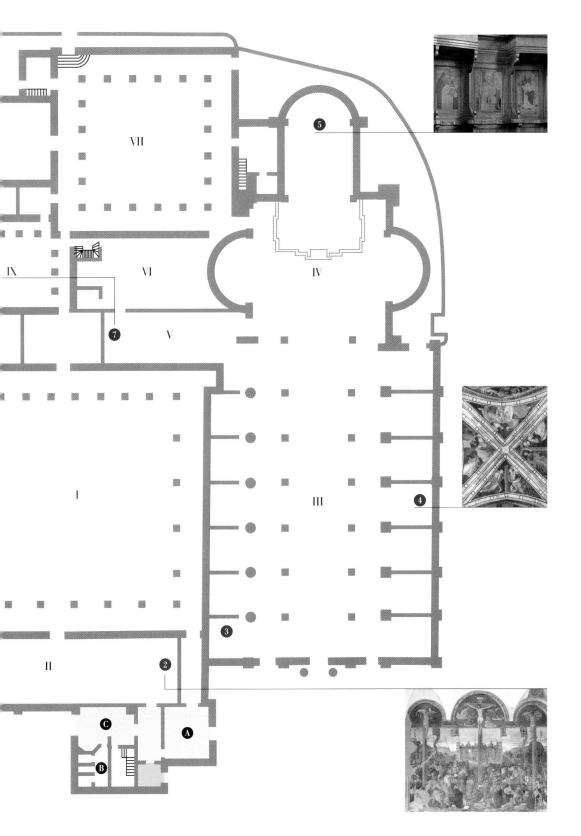

VII

5

IV

IX

VI

7

V

I

III

4

3

2

II

C

A

B

The Restoration of the *Last Supper*

Over twenty years after the beginning of the restoration work, Leonardo's *Last Supper* has been returned to the international world of culture and the public eye in a state of preservation that perhaps it has never been possible to achieve since the sixteenth century. At the beginning of the extremely delicate restoration process we did not have the intention, or labour under the illusion, of bringing back to light Leonardo's painting exactly as Leonardo had left it after putting down his brush for the last time. But we aimed, above all, to conserve the original layers of colour that still — we were certain — had survived the five centuries of its tormented history, and the quality and quantity of what we found far exceeded our expectations. The painting, however, comes down to us in an altered and distorted form, not only because of the length of time that has passed and the vicissitudes it has undergone, but because of past critical readings and interpretations of it, because of the copies made of it, and, last but not least, because of the image of it that has become familiar to the collective memory. Thus, while the fragments unveiled by this restoration still display their age and the "signs" of the time that has passed (which could be described as the historical significance of the painting), the visitor has to make a great effort to link this newly restored work to the "idea" imprinted in his mind (through the numerous popular reproductions and photographs in circulation, which are all touched up and altered to give as complete an image as possible of the picture). The painting is certainly fragmentary, since there are large areas where nothing of the original survives. However, the fragments with their intense, bright colours, linked together by very meticulous, thinner, water-colour additions (so that it is always evident where the original painting finishes and where the areas in which it has been lost begin) now contribute to creating a more reliable image and one that is closer to the lost original than the eighteenth-century repaintings. Apart from altering and distorting the faces, expressions, attitudes and colours, they had also concealed the general effect of the composition for over two centuries, by removing any suggestion of depth, and, above all, by eliminating the extremely balanced play of light and shadow, which today gives the fragmentarily rediscovered painting the tonal equilibrium that Leonardo had used to solve the problem of the relation between chiaroscuro and colour.

In reprinting my text on the *Last Supper* almost fifteen years after it was first published, I have not wanted to alter the content, because this is intended to be a first historically orientated approach to the appreciation and understanding of this famous mural painting. The whole of the first part (which attempts to reconstruct its history and significance) is therefore little changed, whereas it has been necessary to make some corrections and additions to the last part, where the results of the restoration — then in progress and now completed — are referred to. Given that this demanding restoration work was also affected by the duration of the process, and there were noticeable changes in direction and methodology (though the high quality of philological research that had inspired it from the outset was always maintained), which are reflected in the accounts and studies that have accompanied the restoration, a bibliography has been added so that the interested reader can obtain further information. One of the material aspects that the restoration has definitively confirmed, by very recently re-examining the stratigraphy, concerns, for example, the type of medium Leonardo employed. The chemical and physical analyses conducted on samples of paint have established beyond any reasonable doubt that tempera was used, perhaps with a thin layer of oil in some places, on two layers of plaster. From the standpoint of the perspective scheme adopted by Leonardo, the rediscovery of the lines he cut in the upper left portion of the composition, and the definitive reading of the band on the extreme right after the first tapestry as part of a wall depicted in perspective, have confirmed that the artist reproduced an imaginary room wider than the actual refectory, in order to suggest a more scenographic, illusionistic background from which the table and the figures of Christ and the apostles emerge three-dimensionally.

P.C.M.

Leonardo's *Last Supper*

Pietro C. Marani

A sheet preserved in the Royal Library at Windsor Castle, no. 12542r, illustrates Leonardo's early ideas for the *Last Supper*, or *Cenacolo*, in Santa Maria delle Grazie.[1] It shows five figure studies; the largest, at the top of the sheet, represents eight or nine disciples grouped around Christ, with Judas seated on the near side of the table. The scene is set against a wall along which run the corbels of a vault, creating a row of lunettes, just as in the real architecture of the long walls of the Refectory of the Grazie (although there is no reason to think that Leonardo intended to paint the *Cenacolo* on one of these walls — the figures would in fact have been enormous).

The drawing, done with lively, darting pen strokes, is deliberately concise: the features of the heads are barely indicated by blots and crossed dashes marking the brow lines and noses. The second drawing, on the right hand side of the sheet, is on a slightly larger scale and shows the group of Christ, John, Peter and Judas as described in the Gospel of Saint John (13, 21–26): "When Jesus had thus said, he was troubled in spirit, and testified, and said, 'Verily, verily, I say unto you, that one of you shall betray me.' Then the disciples looked one on another, doubting of whom he spake. Now there was leaning on Jesus' bosom one of his disciples, whom Jesus loved. Simon Peter therefore beckoned to him, that he should ask who it would be of whom he spake. He then lying on Jesus' breast saith unto him, 'Lord, who is it?' Jesus answered, 'He it is, to whom I shall give a sop, when I have dipped it.' And when he had dipped the sop, he gave it to Judas Iscariot, the son of Simon."

Leonardo therefore initially chose to portray the moment which had already been represented by artists for centuries, when Christ gives the sop of bread to Judas, thus identifying him as the traitor. As Jack Wasserman has pointed out, among the first portrayals of this episode described by Saint John (in the Gospel according to Saint Luke, the traitor is identified by his hands, which are with Christ's on the table, a scene apparently never painted) there is a relief in the cathedral of Volterra; another, dating from the twelfth century, in San Giovanni Fuoricivitas at Pistoia; and a fres-

Interior of the refectory of the church of Santa Maria delle Grazie

The refectory damaged by bombing in August 1943

*Leonardo, Study for the head
of James the Greater.
Windsor Castle, Royal Collection
(no. 12552)*

*Leonardo, Study for the head
of Philip. Windsor Castle,
Royal Collection (no. 12551)*

*Leonardo, Head in profile
facing right. Windsor Castle,
Royal Collection (no. 12548)*

*Leonardo (with later repainting),
Head of Christ. Milan,
Pinacoteca di Brera*

co of the same century in the abbey of Viboldone, just outside Milan.[2]

But the most striking feature of Leonardo's drawing is the extraordinary detail of Christ's left arm presented in two positions: one outstretched, in the act of taking or handing the bread, and the other withdrawn, in the gesture of pointing or moving towards the plate. This creates a sort of photographic sequence which gives the scene vitality and movement. Added to this there is the reaction of Saint Peter, who shows astonishment and stares at Judas with a severe, questioning look, moving his hand to his forehead. His expression contrasts with that of Christ, who already appears suffering, merciful and resigned. It is quite extraordinary how Leonardo, with a few pen strokes and blots, in a few square centimetres of paper, could concentrate such a great variety of attitudes, movements, expressions and meanings. This makes us regret all the more that much of the great mural has been lost. In the painting, the subtle variations, correspondences and resonances between one character and another must have been much more marked. The Windsor sheet is therefore all the more important, and certainly the most significant among the surviving studies for the painting.[3]

Another series of preliminary remarks suggests itself before we go on to consider Leonardo's masterpieces itself. The sheet discussed here, Windsor 12542, besides other figure drawings connected with the *Cenacolo*, both on the *recto* and the *verso* presents several studies relating to architecture, geometry and mechanics. These drawings confirm the date of the sheet, around 1492–94, and are interesting because they link the studies for the *Cenacolo*, and the painting itself, to a particular period of Leonardo's activity marked by an especially wide range of interests and studies. This was the decade 1490–99, one of the most busy and

Leonardo, Studies for the Last Supper. Windsor Castle, Royal Collection (no. 12542)

stimulating for Leonardo. Besides his work as an artist, in those years he devoted himself particularly to the study of movement and mechanical phenomena, while also elaborating observations and notes which he hoped would develop into a consistent, organic treatise on painting. The result of his studies of mechanics, ballistics, the repercussion of movements, visual rays and sound, and of anatomy as a system of mechanics applied to the human body, is already clear in the Windsor drawing 12542r and is fully reflected in the *Cenacolo*.

In the painting, however, the moment of the Passion which is represented is not the one illustrated in the preparatory studies of the Windsor sheet. We have no documentation of Leonardo's transition from this initial stage, but the moment represented in the mural is the one immediately preceding the identification of Judas, when Christ makes the statement: "One of you shall betray me." These words evoke immediate astonishment and an emotional reaction in the apostles. Peter turns to John inviting him to question Jesus, just as described in the verses from Saint John's Gospel quoted above (and in fact John, rather than lying on Jesus' breast as in the traditional representations of the Last Supper, is sitting back, because Peter has called on him to ask Christ for an explanation). Christ's words, "One of you shall betray me," strike the apostles like sound waves, rebounding from one to another and creating the variety of their gestures, attitudes and movements. It is as though the diagram of a law of acoustics, optics and dynamics[4] had been directly translated into painting. The different reactions of the apostles correspond to the different ways a light ray is reflected and returns, according to the type of surface refracting it. This is confirmed by certain observations of Leonardo's. In particular, there are two passages in a manuscript entirely devoted to problems of light and shade, the Institut de France Ms. C, f. 16r, dating from around 1490, in which Leonardo compares the diffusion of sound and visual rays: "On reflected movements. I desire to define why bodily and spiritual movements, after striking the object rebound at equal angles.

On bodily movements. I say the re-echoing voice is reflected by striking the ear, as objects striking mirrors are reflected to the eye. And just as the image falls from the thing to the mirror and from the mirror to the eye at an equal angle, so the voice, when it first strikes the ear, will fall and rebound at equal angles in the cavity."

Other notes comparing the propagation of sound to that of visual rays, and likening these effects to the diffusion of waves around a point struck in water, can also be found in manuscripts almost entirely devoted to problems of paint-

13

Leonardo, Study for the hands of John. Windsor Castle, Royal Collection (no. 12543)

ing. They appear, for example, in sheets 9v and 19v of the Paris Ms. A, 1490–92 circa; and also Ms. H, sheet 67r[5] and in an older sheet, dating from around 1490, of the *Codex Atlanticus*, 1041r (ex f. 373r-b), which presents the following conclusions: "The stone, where it strikes the surface of the water, causes circles around it which spread until they are lost; and in the same way the air, struck by a voice or a noise, also has a circular motion, so that he who in nearest hears it best and he who is most distant cannot hear it." These words seem to be a literal illustration of the attitudes of the disciples around Christ.

In approaching the *Last Supper*, then, we should also consider the related studies in optics, mechanics and dynamics which occupied Leonardo in the immediately preceding period and during the years when he was working on the painting. The perspectival plan is very much in evidence, but his extreme simplicity in fact conceals another key for understanding the painting. The composition even suggests that circular form which Leonardo always loved as life-propelling and suggestive of harmony. Critics have often noted the grouping of the figures in threes, as though they were governed by a force which expands from the centre of the composition — Christ — outwards, but returns towards its propelling centre just like a refracted wave — the group of three apostles on Christ's immediate left, with James and

Leonardo, Study for the right arm of Peter. Windsor Castle, Royal Collection (no. 12546)

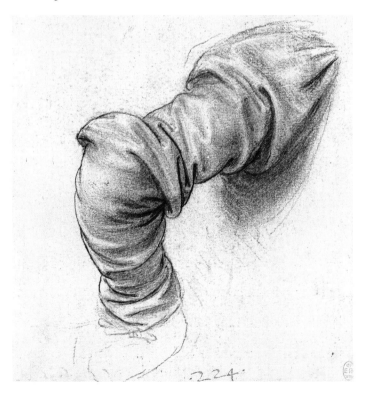

Leonardo, Study for the right foot of Christ. Windsor Castle, Royal Collection (no. 12635r)

Leonardo, Study for the head of Judas. Windsor Castle, Royal Collection (no. 12547)

Thomas leaning towards him. However, this is not the only connecting link between the variety of figures and movements.

The arrangement of the apostles around Christ appears to correspond to a broader, more general plan, in the form of a vast semicircle suggesting an apse. This feeling is conveyed by the greater visual importance of the figures at the ends of the table and the distancing towards deeper planes of the intervening figures. The depth of this great niche seems to be measured by James the Greater's outspread arms and inside it – in a plan it would be a sort of *lunula* – the draped table is exactly placed. Being very long, the table in its turn seems to produce the visual effect of greater height towards the centre, which brings the figure of Christ forward, balancing his backward movement. The disciples thus appear to be arranged like the spokes of a wheel around him, although the axes of the figures present evident variations within this general scheme.

More than in the expressive gestures of the hands, perhaps not altogether free of rhetorical devices, one can note subtle variations in the inclinations of the heads. Only two appear in exact profile, perpendicular to the table – Bartholomew and Matthew, at opposite ends; Simon's head is in *profil perdu*, as though rotating in space, while the others either present a three-quarter view or are slanted with respect to the frontal plane of the painting, in variations that all avoid the orthogonal presentation. Even the second head from the left, which seems to be in profile, should in reality be slightly bent towards the foreground, as can be seen very clearly in the Royal Academy copy (one of the earliest and most faithful). Christ's head, since it emphasizes the vanishing point of the perspective and marks a real spatial depth with respect to the plane of the table, is slightly smaller than the others (about 33 cm high). The heads of the apostles (including those at the ends, Bartholomew and Simon, which appear larger) are all much the same height (36–37 cm approximately). This uniformity in the size of the heads, attenuated however by the foreshortening of those placed obliquely to the plane of the painting, can create a feeling of discomfort, as though they were breaking through towards the frontal plane of the table; for example, the head of Thomas, which should in fact be well back and therefore appear smaller, is larger than Christ's. All this however shows that Leonardo undoubtedly intended to offer a very wide compendium of the *moti dell'anima*, the "movements of the mind" reflected in multiple attitudes and human expressions (his many drawings of caricatural and even "grotesque" heads, where the physiognomical studies are taken to an extreme, probably

Leonardo, central lunette above the Last Supper

derive from his studies for the expressions of the apostles). What other "test," what words other than those pronounced by Christ could so well have illustrated Leonardo's artistic and aesthetic theories? These ideas were explicitly set out in the contemporaneous memorandum of the *Forster Codex* II, ff. 62v-63r[6] and in various notes for the *Treatise on Painting*. There we read, for example: "The movements of men vary with the variety of accidents running through their minds: and each accident in itself moves these men to a greater or lesser degree according to their greater force and age; because the same occurrence will cause a different movement in a young man than in an old one," where the terminology (movements, accidents, greater force, etc.) and the mental process implied are the same applied by Leonardo to the study of the causes of "accidental" or induced movement in mechanics and dynamics.

Assuming that this concatenation of spiritual movements and reactions translated into attitudes and physiognomies is what Leonardo intended to leave to history as the final form of his programmatic manifesto (perfectly matching the visualization of a passage in the Gospels), then the spatial context – the capacity, at first sight rectangular, of the painted refectory in which Jesus and the apostles are sitting – appears as a simple container. The space has been created not so much to give illusory continuity to the real refec-

Leonardo, right and left lunettes above the Last Supper; lunette on the left wall

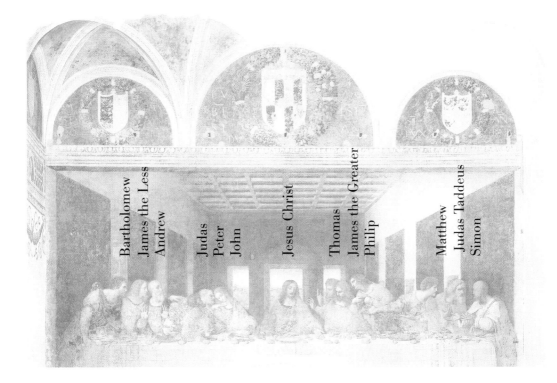

Bartholomew
James the Less
Andrew

Judas
Peter
John

Jesus Christ

Thomas
James the Greater
Philip

Matthew
Judas Taddeus
Simon

Scheme of the Last Supper

Facing page
Leonardo, detail of a lunette

tory (although once that effect must have been much more obvious than today, especially considering the pale tones now emerging and the original lighting of the room),[7] but to accelerate the drama and concentrate the scene on Christ, the main actor in the story unfolding before us. It is Christ who generates all the "movement" in the Leonardian sense ("movement is born of force" – an evident allusion to Christ's spiritual force, remembering the artist's definition: "force is a spiritual virtue"). This clearly foreshadows his later theories referring to the "Prime Mover," God, to which Martin Kemp has recently drawn attention.[8] Christ's word, the Word of God, by giving life to the scene represented, gives life and movement to the whole universe.

After these considerations, the problem of the perspectival construction of the *Cenacolo* appears almost marginal. It may never be finally solved, even after all the incised lines recently discovered in the upper part of the composition[9] have been fully revealed and studied, possibly because it was left deliberately ambiguous by Leonardo himself. He seems to have carefully hidden the few solid reference points which would have allowed a reconstruction of the perspectival scheme (the two painted walls in fact extend beyond the frontal plane of the picture) and has given the room an accelerated perspective rather than the fixed stat-

Leonardo, Last Supper, detail
of the apostles on the left

Leonardo, Last Supper, detail of Christ with the apostles

Leonardo, Last Supper, detail of the apostles on the right

ic perspective of the Florentine tradition, which at that time he was anyway questioning.[10] Rather than the perspectival image of a rectangular room, the result is the contracted image of a trapezoidal container. The problem of perspective cannot in any case be considered separately from the idea and theories relating to the "movements of the mind" which it was Leonardo's chief aim to illustrate, much less be taken as an isolated problem. The architectonic space depicted is used by the artist to test other hypotheses, to check his theories on light and shadow and exemplify them in a form which is in perfect consonance with the diagrams and jottings in the Paris Ms. C.

The painted room behind the apostles is used by Leonardo to experiment with a highly complicated lighting situation. Three different sources of illumination come from the back, mingling like three beams of light shining into an optical box through different openings. And from the left comes a stronger light which Leonardo made more or less coincide with the real light coming through the windows on the left side of the Refectory; finally there is a light coming from the Refectory itself, at right angles – or almost – to the picture plane.

So the wall of the painted room on the left is almost completely in shadow; but towards the vanishing point the shadow should be lessened by the light coming through the windows. The right wall is almost completely illuminated, but the end part is slightly in shadow (a vertical stripe of shade corresponding to the last tapestry in a subtlety which unfortunately has been almost completely lost in the original, but is clearly visible in some copies and even in the Dutertre water-colour). The shadow produced by the part of the back wall beside the first window on the right is lit by the source light which corresponds to that of the real windows. The beautiful drawings of the Paris Ms. C show how behind this differentiated lighting there lie dozens and dozens of studies on proper shadows, "percussed and repercussed," and a passage in f. 14v seems to anticipate the "optical experiment" demonstrated in the *Cenacolo*: "Repercussed shadow is that which is surrounded by lighted wall."

The consonance between what Leonardo has depicted in the *Cenacolo* and his studies of the same period is so exact that I am not convinced, either, by the suggestion that the *Supper* and the gestures of Christ and the apostles should be interpreted as symbolizing the institution of the Eucharist, particularly if this thesis is taken as the sole key to understanding the painting. The moment of the sacrament precedes the revelation of the betrayal and certainly does not demand such an emotional and dramatic reaction as we

see here in the movements and attitudes of the apostles. Saint Mark (14, 22–25) says that: "And as they did eat, Jesus took bread, and blessed, and brake it, and gave to them, and said: "Take, eat: this is my body.' And he took the cup, and when he had given thanks, he gave it to them and they all drank of it. And he said unto them, 'This is my blood...'" In the painting the apostles are neither eating nor drinking nor receiving the blessing, and Christ is not making the gestures described by Saint Mark. Finally, not even Simon's attitude, on the far right, indicates that he is receiving the bread and the wine, as has been claimed after the restoration.[11] Rather than making a "ritual" gesture, he is simply holding out his hands to question, or to question himself without finding an answer ("the other with hands outspread shows their palms... and his mouth expresses amazement" – the description refers to the third apostle from the right, Andrew, but explains his gestures in terms of the astonishment aroused by Christ's words).

Heydenreich accepts the simultaneous existence in the painting of an allusion to the institution of the Eucharist, but considers it a significant addition, and only after having greatly insisted on the fact that the episode depicted by Leonardo is the moment immediately prior to the announcement of the betrayal.[12] Reservations about Steinberg's hypothesis had already been expressed by Anna Maria Brizio.[13]

On the other hand, one simply cannot believe that the scene represents an image blocked like a photogram at a moment which carries a single meaning: the painting is rich with significances and symbolic allusions, and the institution of the Eucharist is one of them. The traditional subject of the *Last Supper* was the most suitable theme to be portrayed in a refectory; but Leonardo, besides the results of more than a decade of studies and experiments, put into it other references and suggestions connected with the Passion of Christ: the offer of self-sacrifice, for example, indicated by the bread and wine, is connected to the *Crucifixion* painted on the opposite wall of the Refectory by Montorfano, and even Christ's position (we should imagine that his feet can be seen, before the door was opened in the wall below) alludes directly to the Crucifixion, with the arms outspread and the feet – as shown in a drawing at Windsor – slightly overlapping. At the same time the bread and the wine, material food for the friars of the Grazie seated at their meal, become their spiritual nourishment after the cycle of the Passion has been completed. Nor can we exclude symbolical meanings in the swags of fruit and leaves which hang above the scene, filling the lunettes. The lunettes are like screens set up between the painted

Leonardo, Last Supper, detail of the table laid for the Last Supper

composition and the real space of the Refectory. They skilfully conceal the point where the wall meets the vaulted ceiling, originally painted in blue with gold stars, which must certainly have created a strong contrast with the illusory coffered ceiling of the mural.

In the central lunette, where the inscription alludes to Ludovico and Beatrice d'Este, dukes of Milan,[14] the garland encloses a coat of arms with contrasting quarters in a chequered pattern. On the dark fields, made of thin silver leaf, the Sforza snakes are painted in bright blue, with typically Leonardesque taste and sensibility. This and the other lunettes were to have been completed by gilding in the ribbons and coats of arms, to strengthen the impression of real shields hanging on the walls (on the opposite wall, the warriors' helmets painted by Montorfano are in relief, simulating metal armour). The garlands as well, particularly the one in the centre, strongly suggest *trompe l'œil*, and their use is certainly connected with the tradition of adorning the fronts of churches and palaces with real wreaths of leaves (as is still done at Easter, for example, on the façade of Saint Mark's in Venice). In Milan it was also custom to decorate palaces with festoons of this sort; Barbara Fabjan has drawn attention to Gian Galeazzo's betrothal to Isabella of Aragon in 1489: the walls of the Castle were adorned with "swags of ivy and laurel made in the antique style" and along the streets were hung "swags of greenery, ornamented with juniper, laurel and ivy," with the ducal insignia. Inside the shield of the coat of arms the recent restoration has

Leonardo, Last Supper,
detail of the face of Christ

Facing page
Leonardo, Last Supper,
detail of the hands of Philip

revealed the first outline, in the shape of a bucrane. This is the motif used in a drawing at Windsor Royal Library, no. 12282a-r, in a study for a Sforza emblem in Ms. H in Paris, and also in a tondo placed outside the apse of Santa Maria delle Grazie representing another "ducal motif."[15]

The epigraph in the left hand lunette refers to the eldest son, Massimiliano Sforza, in his earldoms of Angera and Pavia,[16] while in the right lunette Ludovico and Beatrice's second son, Francesco II, born in 1495, was to have been celebrated as Duke of Bari; his name however does not appear.[17] The recent restoration indicates that in several points leaves and fruits have been repainted, as can also be deduced from an interesting series of photographs taken by ultraviolet and infrared radiation, a sequence of which is published here. The design is certainly Leonardo's. This is particularly clear in the drawing of the beautiful waving ribbons, a number of lanceolate leaves in the left lunette, the blue snakes already mentioned, and from the general composition. However, the brush stroke seems too heavy and loaded, and the colour in several points is dull despite the exceptionally good state of preservation of the leaves and of several groups of fruit. Nevertheless, laboratory examinations seem to indicate a technique of execution identical with that of the *Cenacolo* below, with the difference that the artist or artists painted (apparently with tempera and an oily binding) directly on a coating of *intonaco*, without the white lead ground used in the *Supper*. The exceptional state of preservation is due to the fact that the lunette paintings

33

were brought to light only in 1854, after four coats of plaster had been removed. According to Ottino Della Chiesa, the lunettes had been subjected to a "ruinous washing,"[18] perhaps in the eighteenth century, and it could therefore be supposed that both the repainting and the subsequent covering over were done at a recent date. However, the decorations seem much earlier; in this case one could suppose that they were covered immediately after the fall of Ludovico il Moro, that is to say after 1499, as a sort of *damnatio memoriae*, to remove the Sforza names and possibly replace them with those of the King of France. It could also be suggested that when Leonardo returned to Milan in 1506, he or one of his pupils reworked the leafy decorations (and certain groups of leaves are stylistically similar to the vegetation that appears in the second version of the *Virgin of the Rocks*), touching up the parts that had fallen or been damaged. It would have to be supposed that the three lunettes were then covered over, since the first mention so far discovered of the existing decorations dates back only to Giuseppe Mazza, in 1770.[19]

In Northern Italian painting, as well, motifs of swags and garlands had a long and illustrious tradition: we need only recall Mantegna's decorations in the Camera degli Sposi at Mantua, or paintings by Carlo Crivelli such as the *Madonna della Candeletta* in the Brera Gallery. Leonardo's choice of this motif is therefore not surprising; and his interest in vegetation is testified by a large number of extremely sensitive botanical drawings which show his extraordinary perceptiveness in rendering the world of plants. The first two lunettes of the long walls in the Refectory also seem to have been decorated by Leonardo. Only the brush drawing in the first lunette on the west wall survives (the one on the east side was destroyed, together with the whole wall, in the 1943 bombing). After its recent cleaning Carlo Bertelli confirmed it as an autograph drawing.[20]

It is correct to suppose that Leonardo began working on the preparatory studies for the *Cenacolo* in the first half of the final decade of the fifteenth century. The enlargement and decoration of the Refectory of the Grazie was part of a wider programme designed to celebrate the Sforza dynasty and Ludovico il Moro in particular. The new apse of the church, built to Bramante's design from 1492 onwards, was the most important and significant work executed in this context. Intended to hold the tombs of Ludovico and his wife by Cristoforo Solari, now preserved in the Certosa of Pavia, the monumental complex must have appeared as a sort of mausoleum, invested with theological and religious meanings beyond its symbolic and celebrative purpose.[21]

The contribution by Bramante and Leonardo to this gener-

Leonardo, Last Supper, detail of the figure of Andrew

Leonardo, Last Supper, detail of the figure of Judas

al programme are further connected by assonances between the architectural ideals expressed by Bramante and the new, monumental scale adopted by Leonardo for the figures of the *Supper* which also seems to refer to an architectural, or even directly Bramantesque idea (compare the figure of Simon with those of the *Men at Arms* of Casa Panigarola, now at Brera). The illusionistic motif of Leonardo's painted architecture recalls Bramante's fake choir in the church of San Satiro, although the blatantly scenographic intentions of the later are, as we have seen, ultimately a secondary purpose in Leonardo's mural. And in 1495 Donato Montorfano had finished his *Crucifixion* on the wall opposite to the *Cenacolo*, although this seems to have been commissioned by the Dominican friars of Santa Maria delle Grazie.

Ludovico il Moro's personal interest in Leonardo's *Supper* is attested by a letter to Marchesino Stanga asking the latter to solicit the artist "so that he may finish the work begun in the Refectory of the Grazie and subsequently attend to another wall of this Refectory." The letter, dated 29 June 1497,[22] besides providing supporting evidence for the idea that Leonardo was also commissioned to decorate the wall that Montorfano had finished painting only two years earlier, also gives a first chronological peg for the conclusive phase of Leonardo's work. The *Last Supper* was certainly finished in the following year, 1498, as Luca Pacioli states in the famous passage, already quoted, from his *De divina proportione*.[23] To date the beginning, one must remember that time was certainly needed to work out the theme and we know nothing of the intermediate drawings between the early studies of the Windsor sheet, already discussed, and the drawings of the apostles's heads, which belong to the final stage of preparation. This, and even more the painting technique chosen by Leonardo (not *buon fresco*, which would have required a rapid, immediate execution, but a technique which would allow him to add further touches later, as Matteo Bandello recalls in his famous story)[24] indicate a year around 1494, if not earlier, as the starting date for his work in the Refectory.[25]

The scientific observations and theoretical notes on painting which I have quoted are from manuscripts datable between 1490 and 1494, which seems to confirm this chronology. Moreover, insufficient attention is usually given to Bandello's testimony as an element for dating the *Cenacolo*. Speaking of how Leonardo often went to the Grazie to paint the *Supper*, he refers to the equestrian monument to Francesco Sforza: "I have also seen him, according to how the caprice or impulse took him, set out at midday, when the sun is in Leo, from the Corte Vecchia where that marvellous clay horse stood, and come straight to the Grazie and, climbing on the scaffolding, take the brush and give a few strokes to one of the figures, then immediately leave and go elsewhere."

It would be very interesting if we could establish what stage of the Sforza monument Bandello is alluding to, since we know that Leonardo had returned to his studies for the horse in 1490 (after probably starting on the project in 1482–83), while the *Codex 8937* of the Biblioteca Nacional of Madrid mentions the final studies for a second version, the finishing of a clay model and, finally, the relative casting in 1493: "20th of December 1493... I finished casting the horse without the tail and on its side." In order for the horse to be cast, however, the clay model must have been finished some time earlier, because in the revolutionary method invented by Leonardo the wax model was to be obtained from the clay model piece by piece.[26] It must be noted that according to Bandello, Leonardo was working simultaneously on the clay model and the *Cenacolo*; since work on the "great horse" seems to have been stopped during 1494–95 ("I will say nothing of the horse because I know the times")[27] and since the "few strokes" Bandello talks about can only refer to a very advanced stage of the work of the *Supper*, we must suppose that Bandello was referring to a period closer to 1492–93 than 1494–95 (a remark about the Cardinal of Gurk's visit, which took place in 1497, precedes Bandello's mention of the clay model for the horse, but this cannot be used to date his description of Leonardo's habits).

Only twenty years after it had been completed, the painting already began to deteriorate: Antonio de Beatis, who visited the *Supper* in 1517–18, found it "very excellent, although it is beginning to be spoiled, due either to the dumpness of the wall or to some other accident."[28] Fifty years later the situation must have become much more serious, creating the mistaken idea that the cause of the decay was an imperfect execution. The Aretine Vasari does not fail to say this spitefully, stating that the work "was so badly done that nothing can be seen any more but a faded smudge."[29] Lomazzo tries to improve matters and justify the master by affirming that the painting was done in oil on an unsuitable *imprimitura*. With Armenini, who found it "half spoiled although most beautiful" we see the beginning of a fashion for decaying masterpieces foreshadowing the Romantic ideal. Subsequent judgements, from Scannelli's (1642) to the accounts by Lattuada (1738), de Brosses (1738), Bartoli (1776) and Domenico Pino (1796), are interlaced with criticisms and problems of methodology raised by the first documented attempts at "restoration," by

Michelangelo Bellotti in 1726 and Giuseppe Mazza in 1770 (although it is not impossible that traces of earlier interventions may be found).

The first intervention was alternately praised and criticized (particularly by Bianconi, 1787) because Bellotti did a number of reworkings in tempera or gouache and revarnished the whole wall in oil (this at least hiding the original painting under his interventions, which however seem to have spared the figures of Judas, Peter, John and Christ). Mazza set himself to remove Bellotti's repainting, using a scraper and filling in the gaps with an oil mixture, particularly on Bartholomew and, to a lesser extent, on James and Andrew.[30]

A careful inspection carried out by Andrea Appiani in 1802 identified the dampness of the wall as the cause of the fall of painting and recognized the impossibility of transferring the mural altogether. In 1821 Stefano Barezzi made an attempt, limited to the area of the tablecloth under the figures of Bartholomew and Christ, to see whether a transfer could in fact be made by consolidating the painting with glue and adding coloured waxbased stuccoes. In 1853–55 Barezzi intervened on the whole surface, consolidating and cleaning it (it was Barezzi, as already mentioned, who removed the plaster concealing the decorations in the lunettes).

A publication by Pinin Brambilla Barcilon shows some remarkable photographs of these early interventions: one can see Bellotti's repainting of Thaddeus' eyes and the table-cloth decorations, and Barezzi's incisions on the table and the flattened picture surface in the areas where he tried to strip off the painting, areas which were then filled with a wax-based material.[31]

The restorations of this century, finally done using physical analyses of the environmental conditions and the chemical components of the painting, allowed the picture to be consolidated as far as possible. Cavenaghi in 1908 established that the *Cenacolo* had been executed in tempera on two layers of preparation. Silvestri, in 1924, did a new cleaning and a new consolidation (applying plaster round the edges of the painted ground). After the bombing of 1943 and the consequent reconstruction of the Refectory east wall, it seemed that every preceding effort to preserve the mural had been in vain. So much dust and condensed humidity was produced by the rebuilding of the wall and floor that Wittgens found the painting darkened and dimmed: "Instead of somewhat white, it appeared completely black... the surface of the *Cenacolo*, swollen with humidity, looked like a rubbery fabric and at the least touch not only the paint but also the underlying chalk priming came away..."[32]

Facing page
*Leonardo, Last Supper, detail
of the figures of Thomas,
James the Greater, and Philip*

Ettore Modigliani, the Superintendent of the time, therefore invited Mauro Pelliccioli to attempt a new consolidation of the painting surface, "to be done more radically than the previous work by Cavenaghi and Silvestri." In 1947 Pelliccioli began to fix the flakes of paint to the plaster by brushing on de-waxed shellac dissolved in alcohol and injecting casein behind it. The shellac gave the paint cohesion, consistency and a lively colour again, so it was possible to go on to the next stage. In 1951–52 and 1954 Pelliccioli worked at recovering Leonardo's original painting. Wittgens pointed out early on that Pelliccioli had intervened particularly where "the eighteenth century colours had hidden the brilliant treasure of Leonardo's own painting." Pelliccioli's cautious and limited cleaning, while achieving extraordinary recoveries – the Assisi embroidery on the tablecloth, the blue of Judas' robe decorated with Cufic letters in gold – stopped short of removing all the old repainting. Pinin Brambilla remarks that "one notes a greater care, in fact, to remove the repainting on the flesh, while the reworking of the eyes and the dark outlines round the faces and hands remain, and he has not insisted on removing the stratifications deposited on the abrasions or in the gaps to avoid making the picture unintelligible."[33] On entire areas, therefore, the repainting was not removed, including the coffered ceiling, the walls with tapestries and the part below the table.

The restoration which has just been finished, was made necessary by a worsening of the environmental conditions of the Refectory and the wall during the sixties and seventies, when a thick layer of dust and smog was deposited on the painting. Preliminary examinations for a new cleaning were begun in 1976 under the guidance of the Soprintendenza per i Beni Artistici e Storici di Milano, then directed by Franco Russoli. He was succeeded by Stella Matalon, Carlo Bertelli, Rosalba Tardito and Pietro Petraroia (since 1993 with my collaboration) who have been supported by the skill of Pinin Brambilla Barcilon. Thanks to the progress of scientific and technical knowledge, it has been possible to make analyses and examinations covering the chemical, physical, environmental, static, structural, and climatic conditions, besides an exhaustive and detailed photographic documentation.[34] This work has been done under the supervision of the Istituto Centrale del Restauro. At the same time a restoration methodology has been perfected and applied which aimed to recover all that remains of Leonardo's own painting, removing the repaintings, old and new, which have to a large extent concealed it up to now. The sections that were repainted have not, however, all been removed. The coffered ceiling remains an eigh-

teenth-century reworking (although a small section of the original has been brought to light on the right), and so do the tapestries, however, on the left, under the heavy eighteenth-century repainting, bunches of flowers belonging to the original design were found. The very damaged head of Judas has been left in its eighteenth-century form, though recent layers of colour have been removed and it has been rendered closer to the original profile. However, this was not a purely aesthetic criterion of restoration: the repaintings, the layers of grime, the mould, the different materials accumulated over the painting during the centuries, have threatened the complex and already delicate mechanical situation produced from the outset by Leonardo's choice of technique. Problems include areas of cleavage, the fall of flakes of paint and ground, and variable reactions of humidity and heat.

The courageous pursuit of this restoration methodology has permitted the recovery of pictorial fragments that, for the very first time, enable us to see Leonardo's "original" painting (though in a fragmentary state of preservation that has been jeopardized by the nine previous restorations) and, in particular, his colours.[35] The figure of Simon on the extreme right has regained its volume and monumentality (closer to Bramante than to Michelangelo) and its iridescent lilac and white tones. Fully revealed in Matthew are the noble profile and wave of emotion pervading him, and the intense, brilliant blue of his tunic. Other elements which have emerged are the grieved but not pathetic expression of Philip, and the deep plasticity of James the Greater's face in its three quarter view with the repressed sigh of amazement that seems to issue from his mouth, with none of the caricatural emphasis of the corresponding Windsor drawing. After dwelling on these portions of the painting – which, though only a few surviving fragments, are of an extremely high quality and imbued with an astonishing light that seems to regenerate even the surrounding areas where only the ground appears – and observing the parts on the left where the heads of Bartholomew, Andrew, Peter and John have been restored (nearly all of them had been enlarged and distorted by previous repainting), the meticulous work, which has "freed" the painting that was bridled, almost obscured, by previous reworking, is clearly evident. The beautiful heads of Bartholomew and James the Less – almost ancient profiles – have been restored to their original design and part of their former beauty, and act as a counterpoint to that of Matthew.

[1] Cf. K. Clark, *The Drawings of Leonardo da Vinci in the Collection of Her Majesty the Queen at Windsor Castle*, second edition revised with the assistance of C. Pedretti, London 1968–69, vol. I, pp. 99–100.

[2] Cf. J. Wasserman, "Reflections on the Last Supper of Leonardo da Vinci," in *Arte Lombarda*, 66, no. 3, 1983, p. 19–20, figs. 6–8.

[3] Among the other preparatory studies, there are the sheets from Windsor Royal Library, nos. 12551 and 12552 (the heads of Philip and James the Greater), 12546 (Peter's right arm), 12543 (John's hands) and 12635r (Christ's feet); doubts have been raised concerning the autography of sheets no. 12547 (Judas' head, which however it seems should be considered authentic), 12548 (the head of Bartholomew or, according to Berenson, that of Matthew; the drawing is almost universally accepted as an original; the doubts about the autography have been raised recently by Carlo Pedretti), 12549 and 12550 (which are in fact copies after a drawing by Leonardo for the head of Simon), 12544 and 12545 (copies of drawings for the hands of Matthew and Thomas). For all these sheets, cf. K. Clark, *op. cit.*, pp. 100–2 and 133, and for other related studies, see the recent catalogue by C. Pedretti, *Leonardo - Studi per il Cenacolo*, Milan 1983, *passim*. Amongst the preparatory drawings for the *Last Supper*, I do not consider the sheet in the Accademia of Venice suspected of being a counterfeit (cf. A.M. Brizio, "Lo studio degli Apostoli nella Cena dell'Accademia di Venezia," in *Raccolta Vinciana*, XVIII, 1959, p. 45 ff., and XX, 1964, p. 414) although more recent opinions seem to rehabilitate it (cf. C. Pedretti, *Leonardo da Vinci inedito - Tre saggi*, Florence 1968, pp. 56–60; Luisa Cogliati Arano had accepted it as a counterfeit in her catalogue of the Venice drawings in 1966, but now seems uncertain: cf. L. Cogliati Arano, *I disegni di Leonardo e della sua cerchia alla Gallerie dell'Accademia*, Milan 1980, pp. 56–57). The drawing was probably begun by Leonardo, who wrote in the names of the apostles himself, but has been largely reworked by a Milanese artist who was much less skilled than the master. A comparison suggests itself with the famous drawing of the *Head of Christ* at the Pinacoteca di Brera, recently proposed again as an original drawing by Leonardo subsequently altered by one or more hands (cf. P.C.

Marani, in D*isegni lombardi del Cinque e Seicento della Pinacoteca di Brera e dell'Arcivescovado*, Florence 1986, pp. 27–31).

[4] Cf. P.C. Marani, "Leonardo dalla scienza all'arte" - Un cambiamento di stile, gli antefatti, una cronologia," in *Fra Rinascimento, manierismo e realtà - Scritti di storia dell'arte in memoria di Anna Maria Brizio*, Florence 1984, p. 44.

[5] Published by A.M. Brizio, *Scritti scelti di Leonardo da Vinci*, Turin 1952 (1966 edition, pp. 252–54).

[6] Cf. J.P. Richter, *The Literary Works of Leonardo da Vinci*, Oxford 1883 (1970 edition, paragraphs 665 and 666).

[7] The theory that the stationary point chosen by Leonardo for the perspectival construction of the *Supper* coincides with the real view of the spectator has been abandoned after the discovery that, in reality, the perspectival point of view is situated about four metres above the original level of the floor of the room. For the most recent studies on the perspective of the *Cenacolo*, see the bibliographical note added to the new edition of A.M. Brizio, *Leonardo da Vinci - Il Cenacolo*, Florence 1983.

[8] M. Kemp, *Leonardo da Vinci - The Marvellous Works of Nature and Man*, London 1981, pp. 261–329.

[9] Carlo Bertelli mentions it in the first reports of the restoration in progress: cf. note 35.

[10] On Leonardo's recovery of mediaeval optics, see the fundamental essay by A.M. Brizio, *Razzi incidenti e razzi refressi (III Lettura vinciana)*, Florence 1963.

[11] C. Bertelli, in L.H. Heydenreich, *Invito a Leonardo - L'Ultima Cena*, Milan 1982, p. 8. The thesis according to which Leonardo depicted the institution of the Eucharist goes back to von Einem and has been more recently reproposed by L. Steinberg. This thesis is rejected by others, including A. Ottino Della Chiesa (*L'opera completa di Leonardo pittore*, Milan 1967, p. 8), who usefully draws attention to a passage by Pacioli in his *De divina proportione*: "It is impossible to imagine the Apostles more attentively alive to the sound of the voice of the ineffable truth when it spoke: 'Unus vestrum me traditurus est.' With actions and gestures from one to another, with vivid and pained amazement they seem to speak to each other, so nobly did our Leonardo arrange them with his graceful hand" (1498). To this should be added the earliest engravings, attrib-

uted to Zoan Andrea or to the Master of the Sforza Book of Hours, where the words with which Christ announces the betrayal appear in a label (one of these engravings is reproduced, for example, by L.H. Heydenreich, *op. cit.*, p. 103; others in C. Alberici, M. Chirico De Biasi, *Leonardo e l'incisione*, Milan 1984, pp. 59–61).

[12] L.H. Heydenreich, *op. cit.*, pp. 41–48.

[13] A.M. Brizio, "Il Cenacolo," in *Leonardo - La pittura*, Florence 1977, pp. 106–107.

[14] The inscription "LV[dovicus] MA[ria] BE[atrix] EST[ensis] SF[ortia] AN[glus] DVX [Mediolani]" now appears in white beside the arms and the garland, against the red ground of the priming.

[15] Cf. C. Pedretti, *op. cit.*, pp. 86–91.

[16] "Ma[ria] M[a]X[imilianus] SF[ortia] AN[glus] CO[mes] P[a]P[iae]."

[17] "SF[ortia] AN[glus] DVX BARI." Francesco II received the title of Duke of Bari in 1497. This date is generally taken as an inclusive limit for dating the lunettes, which are therefore traditionally supposed to have been executed between 1495 (birth of the second son) and 1497 (bestowal of the title of Duke of Bari). This dating put forward for the lunettes does not however contradict what is said further on about the possibility of anticipating the date of the beginning of the *Cenacolo*.

[18] A. Ottino Della Chiesa, *op. cit.*, p. 99.

[19] Cf. B. Fabjan, "Il Cenacolo nuovamente restaurato," in *Leonardo - La pittura*, Florence 1985, p. 93, note 1.

[20] C. Bertelli, *op. cit.*, pp. 12 and 145 (plate).

[21] See the essay by S. Lang "Leonardo's Architectural Designs and the Sforza Mausoleum," in *Journal of the Warburg and Courtauld Institutes*, vol. XXXI, 1968, pp. 218–33. Also see M. Rossi, "Novità per Santa Maria delle Grazie di Milano," in *Arte Lombarda*, 66, 1983, pp. 35–70, and for other connections, P.C. Marani, "Leonardo e le colonne 'ad tronchonos' - Tracce di un programma iconologico per Ludovico il Moro," in *Raccolta Vinciana*, XXI, 1982, pp. 103–20.

[22] The letter is quoted in its entirety in almost all the literature on the *Cenacolo*: see in L. Beltrami, *Documenti e memorie riguardanti la vita e le opere di Leonardo da Vinci*, Milan 1919, pp. 48–49.

[23] Cf. above, note 12.

[24] M. Bandello, *Le novelle*, Bari 1910, vol. II, p. 283.

[25] The Leonardo passage from the Paris Ms. H. f. 64, dated 29 January 1494, presented recently also by L.H. Hey-

denreich (*op. cit.*, p. 32, n. 3) in support of a proposal to date the commission of the *Cenacolo* to 1494, is not probatory, however. In fact, "il pian delle mura," "la sala" and "la ghirlanda" of which Leonardo speaks refer not to the *Cenacolo* but to the Castle of Milan. The correction was recently made by Pedretti, *op. cit.*, p. 70, independently, by P.C. Marani, *L'architettura fortificata negli studi di Leonardo da Vinci, con il catalogo completo dei disegni*, Florence 1984, pp. 139–40.

[26] On the "Sforza horse," cf. M.V. Brugnoli, "Il monumento Sforza," in *Leonardo*, edited by L. Reti, Milan 1974, pp; 86–109.

[27] The mention occurs in a draft letter to Ludovico il Moro in which reference is also made to the commission "to paint the small rooms" in the Castle and which Brizio places before a text of the Paris Ms. H dated 1494. Cf. A.M. Brizio, *op. cit.*, 1952 (1966, pp. 639–40).

[28] L. Pastor, *Die Reise dess Cardinals Luigi d'Aragona*, Freiburg 1905.

[29] G. Vasari, *Le vite de' più eccellenti pittori scultori e architetti*, Florence 1568.

[30] For this and the following information, cf. B. Fabjan, *op. cit.*, p. 93 ff., note 1.

[31] P. Brambilla Barcilon, *Il Cenacolo di Leonardo in Santa Maria delle Grazie - Storia, condizioni, problemi*, Milan 1985, fig. 1, pp. 15–19.

[32] F. Wittgens, "Restauro del Cenacolo," in *Leonardo - Saggi e ricerche*, edited by the "Comitato Nazionale per le Onoranze a Leonardo da Vinci nel quinto centenario della nascita," Rome 1954, pp. 3–4.

[33] P. Brambilla Barcilon, *op. cit.*, p. 66.

[34] See, for example, the report by the Istituto Centrale del Restauro in Rome, dated 20 September 1977; the report by H. Travers Newton of 10 September 1977; the thermohygrometric tests by the Centro "Gino Bozza" of Milan in September 1979; the tests for the pollution of the air in the room of the *Cenacolo* conducted by the Stazione Sperimentale per i Combustibili, Milan, on 18 October 1979, etc., all in Soprintendenza per i Beni Artistici e Storici di Milano, Archivio corrente, 13/31. See also M. Matteini, A. Moles, "A Preliminary Investigation of the Unusual Technique of Leonardo's Mural 'The Last Supper', in *Studies in Conservation*, 24, 1979, pp. 125–33, and the analyses published in *Arte Lombarda*, 62, 1982. Cf. also H. Travers Newton, "Leonardo da Vinci as Mural Painters: Some Observations on His Materials and Working Methods," in *Arte Lombarda*, 66, 1983, pp. 71–88.

[35] See the reports on the first sensational discoveries: C. Bertelli, B. Fabjan, "Il Cenacolo di Leonardo," in *Brera-Notizie della Pinacoteca*, autumn-winter 1981–82, pp. 1–4; C. Bertelli, *op. cit.*, pp. 127–56; C. Bertelli, "Il Cenacolo vinciano," in *Santa Maria delle Grazie*, Milan 1983, pp. 188–95; D.A. Brown, *Leonardo's Last Supper: The Restoration*, Washington D.C. 1983; B. Fabjan, *op. cit.*, pp. 90–94. See also C. Bertelli, "Verso il vero Leonardo," in *Leonardo e Milano*, edited by G.A. Dell'Acqua, Milan 1982, pp. 83–88.

Bibliography

Accounts of the restoration work as it proceeded from top to bottom and right to left, further to the above-mentioned studies, have been given by: P. Brambilla Barcilon, *Il Cenacolo di Leonardo...*, cit., 1984; B. Fabjan in *Leonardo. La pittura*, 1985, pp. 90–94; C. Bertelli, "Leonardo e l'Ultima Cena (c. 1595–97)," in *Tecnica e stile: esempi di pittura murale del Rinascimento italiano*, eds. E. Borsook and F. Superbi Gioffredi, The Harvard University Center for Italian Renaissance Studies at Villa I Tatti, Florence 1986, pp. 31–42; P. C. Marani, "Leonardo's Last Supper: Some Problems of Restoration and New Light on Leonardo's Art," in *Nine Lectures on Leonardo da Vinci*, eds. A. Bednarek and F. Ames Lewis, University of London, London 1990, pp. 45–52; id., "Le alterazioni dell'immagine dell'Ultima Cena di Leonardo dopo le più recenti analisi," in *Kermès. Arte e tecnica del restauro*, III, no. 7, 1990, pp. 64–67; R. Tardito, "Il Cenacolo di Leonardo e il suo recente restauro," in *Raccolta Vinciana*, XXIII, 1989, pp. 3–16; P. Brambilla Barcilon and P.C. Marani, "Le lunette di Leonardo nel Refettorio delle Grazie," in *Quaderni del Restauro*, 7, 1990.

A first photographic report on the righthand section of the composition after its restoration (including the figure of Christ) is published in P.C. Marani, *Leonardo*, Milan 1994 (other editions: Madrid 1995; Paris 1996). The analyses carried out during the recent restoration work have brought to light the medium adopted by Leonardo: tempera (perhaps mixed with oil) applied to two layers of base, the first thicker layer of calcium carbonate, the second thinner layer to which the paint was applied of white lead. See H. Kuhn, "Bericht über die Naturwissenschaftliche Untersuchungen der Malerei des Mailänder Abendmahls," in *Maltechnik*, IV, 1985, pp. 24–51. The most important analyses carried out on the mural painting, the physical and chemical results, and the precautions taken for its conservation will soon be published in a volume edited by G. Basile and M. Marabelli, *Il Cenacolo di Leonardo. Analisi e ricerche*, Milan, 1999. The final report on the restoration and the resulting new information are contained in P.C. Marani and P. Brambilla Barcilon, *Leonardo. L'Ultima Cena*, Milan 1999.

The restoration that has now been completed and began with cleaning attempts in 1977 has raised some comments and criticism. The most serious comes from M. Kemp, "Looking at Leonardo's Last Supper," in *Appearance, Opinion, Change: Evaluating the Look of Paintings*, United Institute for Conservation, London 1990, and "Authentically Dirty Pictures," in *The Times Literary Supplement*, 17 May 1991, to whom P.C. Marani replied in "Lettera a Martin Kemp (sul restauro del Cenacolo," in *Raccolta Vinciana*, XXV, 1993, pp. 463–67. M. Kemp replied to this in "Letter to Pietro Marani (on the restoration of the Last Supper)," in *Raccolta Vinciana*, XXVI, 1995, pp. 359–66. See also J. Franck, "The Last Supper, 1497–1997: The Moment of Truth," in *Academia Leonardi Vinci. Journal of Leonardo Studies and Bibliography of Vinciana*, vol. X, 1997, pp. 165–82.

P.C.M.

The South Wall

Giovanni Donato Montorfano

Crucifixion
1495

On the wall opposite Leonardo's *Last Supper*
there is the vast composition frescoed by Donato
Montorfano, which extends into the spaces of the
lunettes. The presence of a *Crucifixion* and a
Last Supper on the two shorter walls of monastery
refectories is a widespread tradition, and the two
large mural paintings were executed almost at the
same time. However, the importance of Leonardo's
masterpiece tends to make one "forget" this less
advanced though interesting *Crucifixion*. The
scene, rich in figures and descriptive detail, is in
a far better state of preservation than Leonardo's
painting. Unlike Leonardo, Montorfano adopted
the traditional fresco technique which is more
durable and long lasting. The comparison is
rendered even more evident by the now extremely
faint portraits of the family of Ludovico il Moro
added in *secco* on the edges of the painting,
next to the groups of Dominican saints.
The date 1495 and Montorfano's signature are
clearly visible on a stone at Mary Magdelen's feet,
beneath the cross. This is the only work signed
and dated by the artist, who painted it at the end
of his career. The composition reflects the
tradition of the Lombard school and the figures
are arranged in groups around three very tall
crosses. Note particularly, on the left, the closeknit
group formed by the women supporting Mary, a
theme that frequently recurs in fifteenth century
Lombard painting and sculpture, and that also
appears in the *Crucifixion* by Bramantino in the
Pinacoteca di Brera. The walled city of Jerusalem
can be seen in the background, against a rocky
landscape that reflects Paduan influences.
The buildings display "modern" architectural
features, and are almost a tribute to the style
of Bramante, with whom Donato Montorfano
was in direct contact.

The Church and Convent of Santa Maria delle Grazie, from the Foundation to Bramante's Intervention

Roberto Cecchi

The Foundation of the Dominican Monastery

The first stone of the group of convent buildings dedicated to Santa Maria delle Grazie, Our Lady of Graces, was laid on 10 September 1463. This important undertaking came at a critical moment in the life of the Dominicans, when the order of preaching friars was starting a movement of renewal after many years of institutional uncertainty and spiritual decline. The crisis had undoubtedly been caused by internal factors, aggravated by particularly difficult external conditions. The plague of 1348–50 had led to a considerable reduction in the number of friars and the missing members had been hastily replaced by new recruits, probably not fully in harmony with the authentic tradition of the order.[1] It may be noted incidentally that during the plague of 1485, the Dominicans of the Grazie were to send some of their members to the monastery of Santa Maria at Landriano in order to diminish the risk of infection.[2]

The order of Dominican friars had enjoyed a successful expansion since its foundation. Officially formed on 22 December 1216 (the formal bulls of approval were issued by Honorius III), in 1277 the order already had 404 houses (convents), in 1303 582, and in 1358 the number had risen to 642. The rules governing the friars' lives had been exactly set out in the constitutions sanctioned by the general chapter of 1228. Already at this early stage the basic requisites of the convent buildings had been established: "Our friars shall have small and humble dwellings, so that the rooms of a single story shall not exceed the height of 12 feet [4.20 m to 4.56 m depending on the region], the rooms with two stories 20 feet [7.00–7.60 m], the church 30 feet [10.50–11.40 m]."[3]

Similar dispositions are to be found in the Dominican constitutions drawn up subsequently, starting from the regulations of 1240. In fact the rules became stricter, establishing drastic criteria of simplicity particularly for the furnishing and decoration of the churches: "Notabilis superfluitates a choris nostris amoveantur et amodo in nostro ordine numquam fiat."[4] And the *Officio Praefecti*

Church of Santa Maria delle Grazie, main door

49

Previous pages
*The exterior of Santa Maria
delle Grazie and the Refectory*

Operum, the Office for the Supervision of Works, existed to ensure that the regulations were observed, as Humbert of Romans, master general of the order from 1254 to 1263, emphasized in his *Opera de Vita Regulari*. The building was to be inspired by respect for the rules independently of the aesthetic result, and had to conform to the spirit of humility and the principle of solidity: "Debet attendere dilingenter ne fiat aliquod quod superfluitatem aut superbiam praetendat; et ad hoc operam dare quod fiat opera durabilia et humilia, et quod paupertati et religioni consona videantur."[5]

However, it would be difficult to find a real correspondence between the written rules and the building done by the order. Exceptions and derogations appear so normal as to become themselves a consolidated practice, and exemptions for technical and proportional reasons were in fact admitted in the constitutions drawn up after 1228.

This apparently contradictory arrangement, which however produced important building achievements, had its reasons in the apostolic activity of the preaching friars. The Dominicans chose to build their houses on the outskirts of towns, and the work was financed by bequests, alms and donations, a system which protracted the building of the convents for decades (it has been calculated that each settlement required an average of over one hundred years to complete). This meant that the Dominicans had a relationship of interdependency with the social context in which they operated.[6]

Towards the end of the fourteenth century the reform initiated by the master general, Raymund of Capua, imposed absolute respect for the original rules. This return to the early strictness was intended to guard against a further weakening of Dominican influence and denoted an explicit, renewed ambition to affect the life of the urban communities. The initiative came from the two Lombardy provinces.

The foundation of the convent of the Grazie was very much part of this reforming spirit and, as we shall see, it was to prove difficult to reconcile the rules of the order with the demands of the benefactors. In fact, the latter were to prevail once more. The determination to build a new convent goes back to 1459 when a deputation of citizens sent a request to this effect to the vicar of the congregation of Sant'Apollinare of Pavia, and obtained a first temporary seat in Milan in the little monastery of San Vittore all'Olmo (known as San Vittorello) near the Porta Vercellina and the ancient basilica of San Vittore al Corpo. This was the second Dominican house in the Milanese area, creating a situation similar to the one existing in

Florence (Santa Maria Novella and San Marco) and also in Bologna.

The other Milanese seat was Sant'Eustorgio, founded in 1227. However this early settlement, because of a peculiar geographical boundary, depended on the province of Piedmont; this explains the request made to the congregation of Pavia rather than to that of Sant'Eustorgio, as would have seemed more logical.[7]

In 1460 the Dominicans received in donation a piece of land in the same area of Porta Vercellina, on which two modest buildings already stood. The first was a structure with an enclosed courtyard surrounded by four blocks "in the form of wings or porticoes sustained by wooden columns, with rooms and other offices attached"[8] which had originally housed the command and infirmary of the troops of Gaspare Visconti – commander general of the Sforza army and donor of the land – in their winter quarters. This original building was certainly adapted to the friars' requirements, but it may have coincided for the most part with the so-called Infirmary Cloister, situated in the north-west part of the Dominican convent and demolished in 1897.

The other already existing building was the Chapel of the Blessed Virgin of Graces. Inside this small structure the count had placed an image of the Madonna and, as we shall see further on, the building of the whole complex started from this early settlement. The convent had initially been dedicated to Saint Dominic according to the tradition of the order. Changed to embrace the symbolical meaning of the pre-existing chapel, the new dedication was sanctioned by the general chapter of the order held at Ferrara on 10 May 1465.

One year after the foundation stone of the church had been laid in the presence of Archbishop Nardini, on 28 August 1464, construction started on the dormitory.[9] Evidently the modest capacity of the pre-existing accommodation (in the Infirmary Cloister?) was no longer sufficient to house all the friars engaged in the work.

Building proceeded with a certain speed; the convent part was completed in 1469. This was a very short time indeed compared with the decades, or even centuries needed to complete other settlements, as we have seen. It may reasonably be supposed that this favourable situation was due to the patronage of the count, who increasingly appears as the man who decided the building destiny of the convent group.

However, according to the chronicler, not everything went smoothly at all times. As was perhaps to be expected, a total divergence of opinion emerged between Vimercati and

53

the friars ("grave altercatione") about the architectural decisions to be made. The count wanted grandiose results, while the Dominicans wished to build in a fashion that would respect the original austerity of their rules and reflect their position as a reformed order.

Vimercati won. However, it must be noted that the work was entrusted to Guiniforte Solari, an architect of great prestige, deeply imbued with the Lombard tradition and certainly oriented towards a deliberate return to Romanesque building forms, with very few concessions to the new ideas introduced by the Tuscan architects who at that time had already been active in Milan for some years.[10]

The Three Cloisters and the Refectory

Today's Corso Magenta, which runs along the south front of the Grazie church, follows a road which already existed at the time when the conventual group was built;[11] so together with the Infirmary Cloister and Lady Chapel, the street constitutes one of the pre-existing limiting factors in the planning of the complex.

Originally, besides this cloister there were two others: the Chiostro Grande (Great Cloister) and the Chiostro dei Morti (Cloister of the Dead). Around these buildings all the activities necessary to the life of the convent had to be organized. Today we are unable to identify the exact sites of all the functions described by Humbert of Romans in his *Opera de Vita Regulari*. This is mainly due to the many alterations made, the damage inflicted by the last war, and the fact that over the centuries the complex has inevitably lost its original character as a self-sufficient group of buildings. We know that every convent was something like a citadel, carefully organized with all the services necessary to the community, and that a specific site was usually assigned to each function.

For purely practical purposes at least fifteen different functions were distinguished, including a storehouse, infirmary, kitchen, leather workshop, vegetable garden and so forth. In addition, as already mentioned, provision was made for an *Officio Praefecti Operum* to oversee the organization of the construction sites and the maintenance of the buildings.[12]

We have seen that nothing remains of the Infirmary Cloister, demolished at the end of the nineteenth century. Judging from the surviving plans, however, it was the most heterogeneous as far as the use of the rooms was concerned. Very little also remains of the Great Cloister: the original ground plan is intact, but the buildings above it were first badly restored in the nineteenth century and then irremediably damaged during the last war. All that remains of

*Donato Montorfano (attributed),
Decoration of the left wall
of the Refectory*

the ancient fabric is part of the ground floor of the west wing; the wide, vaulted ceiling gives an idea of the importance of the original structure.

The so-called Cloister of the Dead was fully intact until the last war, when it underwent irreparable damage and an unconvincing subsequent reconstruction. However, a fairly complete documentation of the original situation remains in drawings and photographs, many of them published in the book by Agnoldomenico Pica and Piero Portaluppi (already cited several times) which thus becomes a particularly important document.

The cloister has columns in *serizzo* (the name given in Lombardy to a granite-like rock) originally surmounted by cross-vaults. Particularly interesting are the twin corner columns which have a heart-shaped cross-section unconsciously derived from Roman architecture and later used again by Biagio Rossetti for the palace of Ludovico il Moro at Ferrara.[13]

The cloister is a perfect square but presents a curious constructional anomaly: the number of the intercolumns is different on three sides. In fact the north and west arcades have six intercolumns, the east one has eight and the south one only five. To explain this oddity three hypotheses are usually put forward: first, interruptions in the course of building; secondly, the need to give as much light as possible to the chapels in the left aisle of the church and to the rooms of the cloister facing north; and lastly, a complete liberty of practice attributed to Gothic art which is assumed to have been free from any need to respect fixed constructional schemes, unlike Renaissance art with its strict planning criterion.[14]

However that may be, the most important functions of the whole complex were distributed around the Cloister of the Dead. At the south end of the east walk there was the Chapel of Our Lady of Graces (part of the present Rosary Chapel). Scholarly opinion unanimously supports the traditional view that this early core gave a direction for the whole development of the conventual group.[15] It seems that the small chapel was not only of symbolical importance, but that it also set the keynote for the plan of the buildings: the walls were continued using the longer side of the chapel rectangle, which thus assumed the important function of a "module." Besides being supported by tradition, this situation is documented by a survey dating from the first half of the seventeenth century in which the original part is marked off from the Seicento building by a wrought iron screen.[16]

Continuing towards the north we find the chapterhouse and the locutory, while the upper floor of this wing, before the wartime destruction, held two rows of cells for the friars.[17] The north side, today completely rebuilt, provided more cells on the ground floor while the upper floor was the site of the library. Besides the surviving drawings, a number of important photographs also testify to the quality of the architectural solutions of late Lombard "Gothic." However, while recognizing that this building has a local flavour, critics have emphasized its Tuscan derivation. In particular, it is usually pointed out that there exists a connection with the architecture of the Dominican library in the church of San Marco in Florence. Malaguzzi Valeri[18] considers that the Grazie library was built by Solari, but directly inspired by Michelozzo's work. This is confirmed by Gattico's chronicle which describes how Count Vimercati, during a visit to Florence, expressed a desire to visit that part of the San Marco building which had been financed by Cosimo de' Medici and designed by Michelozzo.[19]

The west side of the Cloister of the Dead is completely occupied by the famous Refectory, celebrated for Leonardo da Vinci's *Last Supper* painted on its north wall. This is a rectangular hall apparently inspired by some criterion of proportion, since the dimensions of length and width can be reduced to a ratio of about 1:4. The Refectory today offers an image which is a copy of the original because most of the fabric has been replaced during the many rebuildings. In particular, during the last war the roof and east wall were destroyed, and both the *Cenacolo* and Montorfano's fresco on the opposite wall were seriously damaged. It has been remarked that the Refectory hall, like the wing added to the Rosary Chapel, does not harmonize successfully with the space occupied by the church;[20] that the volumes do not "match" as a correct architectural tradition would require. For this reason it has been surmised that in the original plan the church must have had an additional arch, aligning it with the west wall of the Refectory.[21]

Entrance to this hall was to be through two different main doors, both placed in the east wall, the first in the centre and the second towards the north. There also existed a third opening, which is still visible in the centre of the north wall under Leonardo's painting. Originally rather small, it was enlarged in 1652 in a thoughtless alteration that cost the feet of Christ. This door led to the kitchens and was walled up in relatively recent times.[22] The lighting of the Refectory is a question which is still being debated, if not in its general outline, at least in the details.[23] We do not know what the original appearance of this hall may have been. It was certainly not as we see it today. Once again, the disagreement between Vimercati and the friars must have led to considerable modifications during the course of the work.

The choice of the lunetted barrel vault, joined at the heads with umbrella vaults, corresponds to more ambitious ideas which certainly arose later. This surmise is confirmed by an examination conducted by Gino Chierici and a document mentioning the payment of work done to reinforce the structure after the hall had been completed. In particular, the drawing shows openings which have been closed again, placed much lower than those existing in the west wall. The thickness of the surrounding walls also indicates that they were designed to support a much more modest roof, probably in wood.[24] The subsequent change in design must have entailed a series of modifications to handle the greater load represented by a heavier covering with increased thrust. This would have justified the decision to build three buttresses outside, alternating with a system of four tie-beams which is still in place. The expenses for this work were met by Eufrasina Barbavara, the wife of a viscount at the ducal court. In these early and controversial stages of building, the windows on the east side of the Refectory must have been rather small and placed between the frieze and the base of the vault: the single arcade of the cloister and its roof would not have allowed lower openings, as would have been possible in the west wall, during a second stage but before 1495.[25] The considerable alterations made at the end of the sixteenth century also affected this part of the fabric. In order to create a continous second storey gallery round the whole perimeter of the cloister, two buildings had to be erected against the north side of the church and the east wall of the Refectory. This change greatly reduced the light inside the hall, so it became necessary to enlarge the windows on the east side in the same way as can be seen on the west wall. On this side the only completely original window has been preserved: the first on the left as one looks at the wall. The opening was blocked up during the building of the adjacent Inquisition rooms.[26]

The Church Attributed to Solari

The church of the Grazie was built between 1466 and 1482. The latest research indicates that building started from the presbytery, as demonstrated by a series of endowments of chapels inside the church.[27] All this corresponded to an established criterion for the order of construction work typical of convents, related to the need to celebrate religious services as soon as possible, while building was still proceeding.[28] Such a supposition is also confirmed by the tradition developed between 1240 and 1264, according to which a church had to possess a deep apse, a sort of "inner church," which would house the choir. Originally, according to Gattico, the Grazie church should have incorporated the presbytery in the apse, using the chapel of the Blessed Virgin of Graces. In reality, this would have determined a different orientation, along a NNE–SSW axis which was certainly not usual. However, there is no trace of the presbytery. It was demolished a few years after the church was completed to make space for the Bramantesque tribune, as we shall see later. Very few traces therefore remain of the original appearance of this part of the church. In fact we have only a report by Luca Beltrami "testifying" that he demolished the fifteenth century remains of the last buttress during the restoration work he undertook around 1890.

Subsequent investigations in the thirties produced no results. This can be ascribed to the fact that it was regular practice to build on very shallow or almost non-existent foundations. All we have therefore are hypotheses of reconstructions, quite arbitrary, developed by Pica and Portaluppi and published in the only existing description. The authors suggest that the church had a polygonal end, such as is found in a great number of churches built by Dominicans and the mendicant orders in general. The speculation appears somewhat rash considering that this

Domical vault of the choir with graffito on plaster and twelve oculi

type of solution was unusual in Lombardy. It never appears in the thirteenth century and is quite rare in the fourteenth.[29]

The church, essentially intact, is articulated in three aisles and two series of square chapels: seven on the south side, only six on the north side. The ribbed cross vaulting resting on pointed arches appears rather heavy, weighed down by the fresco decorations that cover its whole surface. The structural detail of the main nave also includes "the handling of pendant vaulting and cross arches supported by pilasters resting *in falso* on the capitals of the columns,"[30] according to a solid tradition of mendicant architecture for *chiese-a-sala* (hall-churches).

The stone bosses at the intersection of the cross vaulting

ribs can be divided into two different groups. The first and largest group is distinguished by the plastic emphasis of the modelling, while in the second group the forms are more traditional. "This group includes the last three keystones of the left aisle; the bosses from the second to the fourth span of the left aisle, and of the chapels on this side of the church, with the exception of the sixth. Both series show traces of paint on the stone, usually blue, applied in the concavity. Evidently several masters were active in the Milanese church, and for most of the bosses of the first group at least, they seem to have worked in the context of a single studio or a unified design."[31]

The Corinthianizing capitals are the only concession to the new taste which had been introduced by the Tuscan architects working in Milan in those years: instead of the smooth, lanceolated leaves to be found in the cloisters and library, there are variously modelled leaves and stems. However, the dimensions and proportions of the capitals reflect the local mode, as do the column shafts, where continuity with the Lombard tradition is represented by the smooth protection leaf at the base.[32]

We have only recently acquired a unified overview of the chapels, with their original dedications and the modifications undergone over time, making a systematic reading possible.[33]

The first chapel of the right aisle is dedicated to Saints Peter and Paul. Originally it contained the tomb of Gabriele Fontana, a pupil of Filelfo and a member of the typographical society founded in 1472. In 1539 it was sold to Paolo da Cannobio, and finally in 1606 it passed to the Rainoldi family. In the fifteenth-century boss of the cross vault *Saint Peter Apostle* is depicted; in the corresponding one of the aisle, *Saint Paul*.

The second chapel is dedicated to Saint Bernard, and Filippo Ferruffini was buried there. Absolutely nothing remains of its original architecture. The present tombs date from the end of the sixteenth century.

The third chapel is dedicated to Saint Michael. The original endowment probably dates back to the year 1483 and it contained several tombs, including that of Giovanni Marliani, physicist, philosopher and mathematician, Giacomo Scrosati, and Amorato del Cerreto of the marquisate of Finale Ligure. The boss of the vault depicts the *Annunciation*.

The fourth chapel, dedicated to the Holy Crown, was endowed in 1502 to receive the remain of the rectors of the congregation of that name (founded in 1497 by the Dominican Stefano di Serego, and recognized in 1499). It remained in the possession of the confraternity until 1663.

The fifth chapel is that of Saint Thomas, originally endowed by the Rusca family and subsequently by the Sauli family. In 1541 the latter dedicated the chapel to Saint Dominic "and probably ordered that the tombs which had previously occupied the Chapel of Saint Thomas be removed."

The sixth chapel is dedicated to Saint Vincent, endowed after 1508 by the Atellani family; the decoration, however, dates from the early seventeenth century. A saint on horseback is represented in the boss.

The seventh chapel is that of Saint John the Baptist, endowed before 1513 by Agnese Botta and her husband, Giovan Francesco de Curte.

The eighth chapel is in the south apse of the Bramante tribune; named after Saint Beatrice, it was endowed after 1503. It was built for Bergonzio Botta, an influential member of the ducal court who played an important role in building the portal of Santa Maria delle Grazie church. In the same chapel there are also the tombs of Filippo Borromeo, his wife Apollonia and his son Cesare; on the other side of the altar, that of Giovanni Borromeo, son of Filippo and commander of the ducal infantry, killed by Baldassarre Rho in 1536.

In the choir there is the tomb of Beatrice Sforza Duchess of Milan. The funeral monument, carved by Cristoforo Solari in 1497, was taken down in 1564 in obedience to the decisions of the Council of Trent and moved to the Certosa of Pavia. Beside it were placed the other members of the Sforza family.

The tenth chapel is dedicated to Saint Martin. Originally it also seems to have been used as a sacristy. The *Libellus Sepulchrorum* documents the existence of a number of tombs, including that of Bernardo da Treviglio, thought to have been the painter Zenale, who in his will dated 1522 asked to be buried in Saint Martin's chapel, where the body of his son Girolamo had been placed after his death of the plague in 1520.

The eleventh chapel is dedicated to Saint Louis and placed in the north recess of Bramante's tribune. Marchesino Stanga, secretary to Ludovico il Moro, and his wife Giustina Borromeo were buried there in 1505.

The twelfth chapel is that of the Blessed Virgin of Graces, already mentioned, which became a funeral chapel in 1483 at the death of Giacomo Antonio Della Torre. In the early sixteenth century various other tombs were added, including that of Archiburgo, the French captain of the castle of Porta Giovia, and Cardinal Branda Castiglioni, a figure of great importance in the religious field and as a patron of Lombard Renaissance architecture.

Cloister of the Dead

The thirteenth chapel is dedicated to Saint Dominic. It seems to have been the first to be made available for endowment: perhaps to Gaspare Vimercati himself, who died in 1467, and certainly to his family. Later the chapel passed to the Borromeo family and in 1575, by decision of Saint Charles, it was remodelled by inserting a small coffered dome and lantern designed by Pellegrino Tibaldi.

The fourteenth chapel is dedicated to Saint Peter Martyr and All Saints. The earliest endowment is in the name of Giovanni Maria Visconti and dates back to 1502; in 1515 it was assigned to count Bernardino Mandelli.

The fifteenth chapel is dedicated to Saint John the Evangelist. The endowment dates back to 1491, but is probably earlier and connected with the name of Cicco Simonetta, brother of Giovanni. The latter is portrayed in the boss of the vault together with Saint John, within an inscription reading "Johanno Evangelista D. Iohannes Simonetae."

The sixteenth chapel is dedicated to Saint Mary Magdalene and seems to have been endowed by Antonio Cagnola, ducal secretary, in the first decade of the sixteenth century. In 1532 the right was shared with the de' Capitani family. The fifteenth-century boss shows Saint Mary Magdalene with the phial containing the ointment with which, according to the Gospel tradition, she anointed Christ's feet.

The seventeenth chapel is dedicated to Saints Sebastian and Roch and was endowed by Pietro Landriani and his wife Elisabetta di Gallarate in the first decade of the sixteenth century; Catelliano Cotta, having married a Landriani daughter, was given a burial place there. Almost nothing of the original chapel remains, however, after the damage caused by the last war.

The eighteenth chapel is dedicated to Saint Catherine but is better known as the Bolla Chapel, from the name of the family it was entrusted to from the end of the sixteenth century.

The main façade of the Grazie church is divided into five sections by a row of buttresses. The width, about 32 metres, is almost double the height (19 metres).

The coping in moulded terracotta recalls a very widespread tradition in the Milanese area;[34] in the upper part of each section there is a round opening or oculus, surrounded by the typical *collarino* in white plaster which besides its decorative function served to conceal building irregularities.[35] None of these openings, however, lights the interior of the church; they are practised on the "wind-stop" part of the structure, above the level of the roof, according to a system which was fairly widespread in Emilia and Lombardy in the fourteenth century (the so-called "wind windows" at Lodi and on the church of San Francesco at Bologna belong to this tradition).[36]

In the central section of the façade, above the Bramantesque doorway the only light-giving oculus opens. Below there are four pointed-arch windows surrounded by white plaster *collarini*. Under these windows, in correspondence with the side aisles, there are two rather low doors, which according to Luca Beltrami were not part of the original fabric. As can be seen in an engraving by Cherbuni dating from the mid-nineteenth century, above these openings two baroque portals had been placed removed only after 1895. Finally, the base: this was originally in brick, as at San Pietro in Gessate, and the present finish in granite comes from Luca Beltrami's restoration.[37]

On the south front, facing Corso Magenta, fairly pronounced pilasters divide the façade into seven sections, corresponding to the bays inside the church. Each contains two pointed-arch windows surmounted by a circular oculus. The great roof in *coppi* (curved tiles) is interrupted by a modest strip of wall corresponding to the main nave, perhaps originally picked out by a painted frieze. The structural arrangement of the church as a whole is based on a re-evocation of Romanesque spatial values. This was a model consciously used by certain masters of the Lombard Quattrocento with the aim of making their own building tradition into a style which could compete with the new ideas introduced by the Tuscan architects.

In the interior the various parts are arranged to create the impression of a single space, developed in depth but transversally expanded so that it immediately appears intelligible as a whole.[38]

The use of columns, the almost equal height of the aisles and chapels, and the light coming only from the side windows, all help to delineate a strongly unified space which seems to enclose the spectator. This corresponds to a very early architectural tradition of the mendicant orders, and the Dominicans in particular, known as the *chiesa-a-sala* or "hall-church." The most important "prototype" was the basilica of Sant'Eustorgio, the first Dominican building in Milan.[39] "Restored" as a hall-church by the friars in the twelfth century, its spatial solution was to become a characteristic feature of mendicant architecture.

In the second half of the fifteenth century Guiniforte and Pietro Antonio Solari were the best-known representatives of the tradition which still used archaic motives. It therefore seems quite legitimate to attribute the building of the church to Guiniforte, of whom a ducal decree even says, "ingenium quasi hereditarium et per manus majorum traditum," explicitly referring to a family tradition of Milanese architects. The many buildings which they are known to have designed or which are attributed to them are among the most important examples of Lombard architecture of the period. Compared with the Solari family tradition, the solution of a *sala a gradinatura*[40] ("stepped hall," referring to the slight difference in the roof heights of the central nave and the two aisles) which was adopted for the Grazie church, by widening its horizontal dimension "accentuates its suggestion of a learned medieval quotation;"[41] it is thought to have been derived from the plan of the Carmine churches at Pavia and Milan designed by Bernardino da Venezia.[42]

Ludovico il Moro and Bramante's Intervention

In the years around 1480, the head of the city of Milan was nominally still Gian Galeazzo Visconti but in reality the young count Ludovico was taking the lead in public affairs. Educated "in the humanistic ideals by Francesco Filelfo, he was familiar with the new ideas of Florence, Mantua, Padua and Venice,"[43] so the Grazie church as designed by Solari would certainly not have met his cultural expectations.

The decision to intervene on the façade of the Grazie by building the Bramantesque portal was the first sign of a new climate which ultimately led to the construction of the tribune and the partial destruction of Solari's church. However, when this work was begun the elaborate programme of future interventions had not yet been devised.

The Portal

The portal of the church was built between 1480 and 1490. Ludovico il Moro took a personal interest in arranging for the necessary marble to be brought from the Fabbrica del Duomo in Milan, as appears from a note referring to a consignment "ad perficiendam portam ecclesiae dominae S. Mariae Gratiis extra portam Vercellinam Mediolani." Recent critics, starting from Pica and Portaluppi, tend to exclude the traditional attribution of the doorway to Bramante.[44] In the past it was even thought that Leonardo might also have contributed to the design, since the marble columns are not unlike the culverins in the *Codex Atlanticus*.[45] The lunette of the portal was in fact painted by the Tuscan master, but later the work was destroyed and replaced with a fresco executed by Michelangelo Bellotti in 1729.

It is generally agreed that the portal shows "assonances" with Bramante's work. The execution seems to be typical of local architects influenced by Veneto models, and the names suggested are Rizzo, Leopardi and Coducci.[46]

Vault of the Old Sacristy

The Tribune

Gattico writes: "When Count Gasparo died, Count Ludovico (who seeing the exemplary holy lives and customs of those fathers and because of the warm recommendations made to him by his friend the count before his death, had become strongly attached to religion) conceived the idea — although on learning of it the fathers were greatly disgusted because of their humility — of gradually demolishing all the count's buildings as if he considered them too positive."

On 29 March 1492 the foundation stone of the new tribune was laid. Not even ten years had passed since the Solari church was finished before it was decided to start a new building programme.

Once the tribune was constructed the intention was certainly clear: the original church was to be completely replaced. In a letter to his secretary, Marchesino Stanga, Ludovico wrote that he wanted a meeting among "all the experts to be found in archiecture, to examine and make a model for the façade of Santa Maria delle Grazie showing the aspect and height to which the church should be reduced in proportion to the great Chapel."[47]

The general outline of the full programme is however unknown. We may imagine that behind the project lay a definite desire to express the new current of ideas not only in terms of architecture, but also to reflect the different religious feeling which accompanied Humanism.

In Ludovico's intention the new church was to be the temple-mausoleum which the Sforzas had been awaiting since Filarete's work for Francesco.[48] Essentially, the final result was meant to integrate the two parts — the centric design of the tribune and the longitudinal one of the nave — according to a plan defined by Francesco di Giorgio Martini as "composite" and considered particularly suitable for large churches dedicated to the Virgin.[49]

It would be difficult to say much more about the general configuration of the new church if a remarkable document had not recently been put into a new light. This is a drawing by Leonardo contained in MS. I of the Bibliothèque de l'Institut de France, in Paris, which Pedretti has brought out by a tracing.[50]

This little sketch, accompanied by two inscriptions and a number, seems to refer specifically to the Grazie church and in fact the plan is very much like that of the tribune. Assuming that this drawing reflects the real project for rebuilding the church, it is clear that the structure was to have been radically changed. The longitudinal part, after narrowing to meet the west side of the tribune, was to have been aligned with the walls of the latter, introducing

Following pages
Old Sacristy

evident variations in the Cloister of the Dead as well.

The tribune has a cubic base marked out by four imposing buttresses carrying semicircular arches which support the dome. Two apses are inserted in the north and south sides, while the east side has a cubic bay covered by a vault, recalling Brunelleschi's design for the Sagrestia Vecchia of San Lorenzo in Florence, and that of the Portinari Chapel in Sant'Eustorgio. Where the west side of the tribune is connected to Solari's nave, the greater height of the keystone has required an unusually verticalized adaptation of the preexisting cross-vault.

Concerning the authorship of the work there is some disagreement. Critics generally speak of a "Bramantesque" structure, by which they mean that some involvement of the master can be assumed in the planning, but no direct intervention at least in the executive stage.

Bianconi, at the end of the eighteenth century, already questioned Bramante's role, and this opinion has been shared by the majority of writers who have dealt with the problem. Yet there is almost contemporary evidence suggesting quite the opposite. A chronicle of the early sixteenth century by Giorgio Rovegnatino states: "Ab egregio viro Bramante urbinate architectonicae artis peritissimo erecta est ea tribuna."[51] And in a document preserved in the archives of the Certosa of Pavia one may read: "Note of marbles delivered from the above-mentioned monastery by order of the Duke of Milan to master Bramante engineer, namely 12 columns taken to Vigevano and other marbles for the church of Santa Maria delle Grazie and for the door of the Castle of Milan, at the prices given here."[52] Later, a document of 1756 recalls that "the great dome... was joined to the body of the ancient church by Bramante." So the critics' partial refusal to attribute the work to Bramante is based on stylistic considerations and on other circumstances showing that the architect could not have spent much time on the site. It is certain that between 1492 and 1493, when building had started, Bramante was several times away from Milan and was also busy with other important commissions such as the Canon-House of Sant'Ambrogio.[53]

On the whole, it is thought that Bramante inspired the work and that the execution was entrusted to others. However, there are subtle distinctions. In the interior, many details undoubtedly suggest the master's style. The *tondi* of the arches, for instance, are directly related to those already existing in San Satiro, and the wheel motif with baluster spokes recalls the same Prevedari engraving. Concerning the exterior, Bianconi's comment is still valid: "Although many like to think that the architect of this last part is Bramante [...] it is too commonplace, mean [...] very different from his other works."[54] Similar words were used by Pica and Portaluppi in the forties: "The presbytery and niches have a commonplace decoration of candelabra with rich mouldings and beautiful medallions; the grave austerity of the whole reappears in the lower part, where the triple pedestal creates a dignified, noble motif unquestionably in Bramante's style."[55] The critical evaluation of the two writers is complex and gives a picture that is fragmentary compared with the impression created by the building as a whole. We can therefore agree with Bruschi when he says: "This volumetric organization – excluding probably some separately inserted details like the *tribune morte* (semicircular niches in the drum visible only from outside) and the corner pillars, should therefore be attributed to the same hand that designed the general plan, that is to say almost certainly Bramante; although as at Pavia, and perhaps also in San Satiro, other masters may have worked with him: here, for example, Amadeo and possibly even Leonardo himself."[56]

Another question remains concerning the tribune: that of the colour. In this case, as well, there are at least two different positions. Chierici[57] suggests that the exterior was completely plastered. The other hypothesis, more widely accepted, is that the original solution was similar to the one we see today. In particular it is thought that the original colour of the *intonaco* must have been a "yellow-reddish ochre," harmonizing the new building with Solari's church.

The Chiostro delle Rane (Cloister of the Frogs)
and the Sacristy

The construction of the new tribune made it necessary to readapt all the buildings in the group. In particular, since the rooms reserved for the sacristy in the old church had been demolished, new space had to be found in an adjacent area. A new cloister was designed: a perfect square with five intercolumns on each side, with Corinthian columns and cross-vault roofing. The well organized architecture is decorated with arched lintels in terra-cotta; the keystones have been attributed to Biagio da Vairone.[58] The rectangular Sacristy has a lunetted barrel vault joined by umbrella vaulting at the two heads, a similar design to the one we saw in the Refectory. On the short north side there is a semicircular apse covered by a half-bowl vault. Above the deep entablature there are four large circular openings on the long sides, and one only on the short sides. The terra-cotta decoration has been heavily reworked, particularly during the restoration of 1895–98.

Bernardino Butinone, Blessed
Reginald of Orléans, left aisle

The Cloister and Sacristy are generally attributed to Bramante, although there can be justifiable doubts about this. Bruschi seems to be right when he says: "The Sacristy of the Grazie, taken as a whole, has an aspect that foreshadows certain solutions adopted by Bramante in his first Roman work: for example, in the Refectory of the convent of Santa Maria della Pace."[59]
It is thought that this group of buildings complementary to the tribune was finished by 1497.[60]

The Grazie convent group underwent considerable alterations and additions over the following centuries.
A few of these changes are worth noting here. The campanile, for example, was built around 1510; later, during the restorations at the end of the nineteenth century, it was lowered by about three metres.[61]
In 1559, when the Inquisition Tribunal was transferred to Santa Maria delle Grazie from Sant'Eustorgio, further space became necessary. As we have already seen, new structures were built against the Refectory. When the Tribunal was suppressed in 1785, Maria Theresa of Austria ordered the rooms demolished.
Finally, the so-called "Chiostrino del Priore" (Prior's Small Cloister) is a recent addition, dating from the end of the nineteenth century. It occupies the space remaining between the Bramantesque building and Solari's convent.

[1] A.M. Caccin, "Come nasce un convento," in *Santa Maria delle Grazie in Milano*, Milan 1983, pp. 16–34.

[2] M. Rossi, "Novità per Santa Maria delle Grazie di Milano." Documentary appendix by Z. Grosselli, in *Arte Lombarda*, 66 (1983/3), pp. 40–43.

[3] G. Villetti, "Legislazione e prassi edilizia degli ordini mendicanti nei secoli XIII e XIV," in *Francesco d'Assisi - Chiesa e conventi*, Milan 1982, pp. 23–312. Cf. also G. Villetti, "Prospettive di ricerc sugli ordini mendicanti: il Fondo Libri dell'Archivio Generale dell'ordine dei predicatori," in *Architettura Archivi*, I, n. 1, 1982.

[4] Cf. "Acta Capitolorum generalium ordinis praedicatorum," in *Monumenta Ordinis Fratrum Praedicatorum Historica*, III, 1897, p. 99.

[5] Cf. Humbertus de Romans B., *Opera de vita regulari* (ed. J.J. Berthier), Rome 1889, II, pp. 331–32.

[6] Cf. G. Villetti *Legislazione...*, cit., p. 24 ff.

[7] Cf. A. Pica, P. Portaluppi, *Le Grazie*, Rome 1938, p. 19.

[8] Cf. P.G. Gattico O.P., *Descrizione succinta e vera delle cose spettanti alla Chiesa e al Convento di Santa Maria delle Grazie e di Santa Maria della Rosa e suo luogo e altre loro aderenze in Milano dell'Ordine dei Predicatori*, ms. (eighteenth century), Archivio di Stato di Milano, Fondo di Religione, p.a., Conventi, Milan, cart. 1398.

[9] Cf. M. Rossi, *op. cit.*, pp. 40–43.

[10] Cf. A.M. Romanini, "L'architettura milanese nella seconda metà del Quattrocento," in *Storia di Milano*, Milan 1956, p. 610 ff.: A.M. Romanini, "Le chiese a sala nell'architettura gotica lombarda," in *Arte Lombarda*, III, 2, 1958, p. 52; A.M. Romanini, *L'architettura gotica in Lombardia*, Milan 1964, p. 509 ff.

[11] Cf. A. Bruschi, *L'architettura*, in *Santa Maria delle Grazie in Milano*, Banca Popolare di Milano, Milan 1983, n. 63.

[12] Cf. G. Villetti, *Legislazione...*, cit., pp. 23–31; more generally, L. Gillet, *Histoire artistique des ordres mendiants*, Paris 1912; P.T. Masetti, *Monumenta et antiquitates veteris disciplinae ordinis praedicatorum*, Rome 1864; E. Meersseman O.P., "L'architecture dominicaine au XIIIᵉ siècle - Legislation et pratique," in *Archivium Fratrum Praedicatorum Historicum*, XV, 1946, pp. 136–90; A.M. Romanini, "Architettura monastica occidentale," in *Dizionario degli istituti di perfezionamento*, Rome 1974, I.

[13] Cf. A. Pica, P. Portaluppi, *op. cit.*, p. 34; A. Bruschi, *op. cit.*, p. 47, n. 19.

[14] Cf. A. Pica, P. Portaluppi, *op. cit.*, p. 33 ff.

[15] Cf. *ibidem*, p. 29 ff.; A. Bruschi, *op. cit.*, p. 39 ff.

[16] Cf. A. Bruschi, *op. cit.*, p. 86 ff.

[17] Cf. A. Pica, P. Portaluppi, *op. cit.*, p. 31; A. Bruschi, *op. cit.*, p. 39.

[18] Cf. F. Malaguzzi Valeri, "I Solari," in *Italienische Forschungen*, Florence 1906, p. 83.

[19] Cf. A. Pica, P. Portaluppi, *op. cit.*, p. 23.

[20] A. Bruschi, *op. cit.*, p. 40.

[21] *Ibidem*.

[22] Cf. in general G. Rocco, *Quel che è avvenuto al Cenacolo vinciano - Come si risana il capolavoro*, Milan 1947, pp. 1–19; G. Martelli, "Ricerche e precisazioni sull'ambiente del Cenacolo vinciano, nel complesso monumentale di Santa Maria delle Grazie," in *Notiziario della Banca Popolare di Sondrio*, 18, 1978, pp. 31–49; G. Martelli, "Il Refettorio di Santa Maria delle Grazie in Milano e il restauro di Luca Beltrami nell'ultimo decennio dell'Ottocento," in *Bollettino d'Arte*, n. 8, 1980, pp. 55–72; M.L. Gatti Perer, "Umanesimo a Milano - L'osservanza agostiniana all'Incoronata, Il magnifico Refettorio," in *Arte Lombarda*, 53, n.s., 57, 1980, p. 54; M. Rossi, "Problemi di conservazione del Cenacolo nei secoli XVI e XVII," in *Arte Lombarda*, 62, n.s., 3, 1982, pp. 58–65; R. Cecchi, G. Mulazzani, *Il Cenacolo di Leonardo da Vinci - Guida alla lettura del dipinto e storia dei restauri*, Florence 1985.

[23] Cf. G. Martelli, *Il Refettorio...*, cit., p. 67.

[24] *Ibidem*, p. 60.

[25] *Ibidem*.

[26] *Ibidem*, p. 69.

[27] Cf. M. Rossi, *Novità...*, cit., p. 39 ff.

[28] Cf. G. Villetti, *Legislazione...*, cit., p. 30 Cf. also R. Bonelli, *Il Duomo di Orvieto e l'architettura italiana del Duecento e Trecento*, Rome 1972; A. Cadei, "Si può scrivere una storia dell'architettura mendicante? Appunti per l'area padano veneta," in *Storia dell'architettura mendicante*, Milan 1980; A.M. Romanini, "L'architettura degli ordini mendicanti, nuove prospettive d'interpretazione," in *Storia della città*, Milan 1978, pp. 5–15.

[29] Cf. A. Cadei, *op. cit.*, p. 350.

[30] Cf. A.M. Romanini, *L'architettura milanese...*, cit., p. 611.

[31] Cf. L. Giordano, "La scultura," in *Santa Maria delle Grazie in Milano*, cit., p. 94 ff.

[32] Cf. A. Bruschi, "L'architettura," in *Santa Maria delle Grazie in Milano*, cit., pp. 51–52.

[33] Cf. M. Rossi, *Novità...*, cit., but particularly S. Aldeni, "Il Libellus Sepulchrorum e il piano progettuale di Santa Maria delle Grazie," in *Arte Lombarda*, 67, n.s., 4, 1983, pp. 70–92, to whom I am completely indebted on this subject.

[34] Cf. L. Grassi, "Note sull'architettura del ducato sforzesco," in *Gli Sforza a Milano e in Lombardia e i loro rapporti con gli stati italiani ed europei (1450-1530)*, Milan 1982; also L. Maggi, M.C. Nasoni, "Per l'analisi del repertorio decorativo tardo-quattrocentesco a Milano: l'Ospedale Maggiore," in *La scultura decorativa del primo Rinascimento*, Atti del I Convegno internazionale di studi, Pavia 16–18 September 1980, Rome 1983, pp. 17–27; H.P. Autenrieth, "La lettura coloristica del chiostro canonicale di Novara - Appunti per il mattone a vista e l'incuria di decorazioni semplici," in *Novarien*, 11, 1981, pp. 39–72.

[35] Cf. L. Grassi *op. cit.*, p. 486.

[36] Cf. A. Pica, P. Portaluppi, *op. cit.*, p. 45.

[37] *Ibidem*, p. 46.

[38] Cf. A.M. Romanini, *Le chiese a sala...*, cit., p. 63.

[39] Cf. A.M. Romanini, *Architettura monastica occidentale*, cit., p. 10; A. Cadei, *op. cit.*, p. 341; M. Righetti Tosti Croce, "Architettura e scultura medievale," in *La basilica di Sant'Eustorgio in Milano*, Banca Popolare di Milano, Milan 1984, pp. 45–68.

[40] Cf. A.M. Romanini, *Le chiese a sala...*, cit., p. 52 ff.

[41] Cf. A.M. Romanini, *L'architettura milanese...*, cit., p. 612.

[42] Cf. *ibidem*, p. 610. Cf. also A.M. Romanini, "L'architettura viscontea nel XV secolo - Chiese a sala e ad aula unica, campanili e palazzi quattrocenteschi nel Milanese," in *Storia di Milano*, IV-V, Milan 1955, pp. 661–84; W. Kröning, "Hallenkirchen in Mittelitalien" in *Kunstgeschichtliches Jahrbuch der Biblioteca Hertziana*, 2, 1938.

[43] Cf. A. Bruschi, *L'architettura*, cit., p. 58.

[44] Cf. A. Pica, P. Portaluppi, *op. cit.*, p. 120. Also De Pagave, C. Casati, *I capi d'arte di Bramante da Urbino nel Milanese*, Milan 1870, p. 44; L. Beltrami, "Santa Maria delle Grazie in Milano," in *L'Italia monumentale*, Milan 1910; A. Bruschi, *Bramante architetto*, Bari 1969, pp. 242, 783 ff.; M. Salmi, "Il Cenacolo di Leonardo da Vinci e la chiesa delle Grazie in Milano," in *Il Fiore*, Milan, n.d.

[45] Cf. G. Mongeri, *L'arte in Milano*, Mi-

lan 1872, p. 212; L. Beltrami, *op. cit.*, and M. Salmi, *op. cit.*

[46] Cf A. Pica, P. Portaluppi, *op. cit.*

[47] Cf. *ibidem*, p. 124

[48] Cf. A. Bruschi, *L'architettura*, cit., p. 62

[49] Cf. *ibidem*.

[50] C. Pedretti, "Il progetto originario per Santa Maria delle Grazie e altri aspetti inediti del rapporto Leonardo-Bramante," in *Studi Bramanteschi, Atti del Congresso Internazionale (Milano-Urbino-Roma 1970)*, Rome 1974, pp. 197–203.

[51] A. Bruschi, *Bramante...*, cit., p. 788.

[52] Cf. A. Pica, P. Portaluppi, *op. cit.*

[53] A. Bruschi, *L'architettura*, cit., p. 76.

[54] A. Pica, P. Portaluppi, *op. cit.*, p. 126

[55] Cf. *ibidem*, p. 147.

[56] Cf. A. Bruschi, *Bramante...*, cit., p. 796. For the question of the tribune see the bibliography indicated by A. Bruschi, *L'architettura*, cit., and *Bramante...*, cit.; also C. Saletti, "La fabbrica quattrocentesca dell'Ospedale di San Matteo a Pavia," in *Arte Lombarda*, VI, 1, 1960, which on p. 52 attributes the terra-cotta decoration of the tribune to Rinaldo de Stauris. Recently, for important new aspects, cf. M. Rossi, A. Rovetta, "Indagini sullo spazio ecclesiale immagine della Gerusalemme celeste," in *La dimora di Dio con gli uomini - Immagini della Gerusalemme celeste dal III al XIV secolo*, catalogue, Milan 1983, pp. 104–15; L. Grassi, "Trasmissioni linguistiche dell'architettura sforzesca:

splendore e presagio al tempo di Ludovico il Moro," in *Milano nell'età di Ludovico il Moro*, Atti del Convegno internazionale, p. 45 ff.; M. Rossi, "L'iconografia della città celeste e della beatitudine nella Cappella ducale in Santa Maria delle Grazie a Milano," in *Città di Vita*, XL, 1, 1985, pp. 107–27.

[57] Cf. G. Chierici, "Alcune osservazioni sulla decorazione interna di Santa Maria delle Grazie," in *Rassegna di Architettura*, 12, 1963.

[58] A. Pica, P. Portaluppi, *op. cit.*, p. 205 ff.

[59] *Ibidem*, pp. 213 and 317.

[60] Cf. A. Bruschi, *Bramante...*, cit., p. 800.

[61] L. Gremmo, "I restauri," in *Santa Maria delle Grazie in Milano*, cit., pp. 196–213.

The Decorations

Germano Mulazzani

Since the convent of Santa Maria delle Grazie immediately became very important in the religious life of Milan, its decoration continued with notable artistic results even after the buildings were architecturally complete. After examining the decorative interventions relating directly to the two different building stages of the church and monastery, this chapter will consider, in chronological order, the works of art preserved there, to give the reader an idea of the rich and complex history of the monument.

Frescoes and Graffiti in the Nave and Apse

As soon as building was finished, Solari's church was given a complete and organic decoration in the form of frescoes covering the vaults and walls of the nave and the vaults and piers of the aisles. The frescoes in the body of the church are still visible today for the most part and taken as a whole, they constitute one of the most eloquent and best preserved examples of church interior decoration as it was understood in Lombardy in the second half of the fifteenth century, before the High Renaissance came with Bramante and Leonardo. This ornamentation to some extent followed and emphasized the architecture, but it also introduced new ideas, contrasting with the fully Gothic style of the building. The decorations of the vaulting ribs, the cornices beside them, the *fiammelle* which ornament the vaulting-cells are still in traditional Gothic taste, while the new tendency is expressed by the illusionistic lacunars with rosettes painted in the soffits of the arches, and even more by the foreshortened tondos above the arches of the nave and the painted niches of the pilasters separating the aisle chapels. In the tondos over the arches with their sharp perspective the busts of saints are portrayed. Altogether there are thirteen of them (originally there were fourteen, two for each span, but one is hidden under the great stucco lunette of the seventh span leading to the Lady Chapel). Starting from the entrance door, the busts portray: two Dominican cardinals (unidentified), two Dominican popes (Innocence V and Benedict XI), Saint Catherine of Alexandria and Saint Sebastian. Saint

Giovanni Demio, Crucifixion, detail

Catherine of Siena and Saint Antoninus, Saint Vincent Ferreri and Saint Dominic, Saint Thomas of Aquinas (identification uncertain) and Saint Peter Martyr; and finally Christ, to whom should have corresponded on the opposite wall the bust of the Virgin.[1]

In the painted niches in front of the aisle piers, saints and blessed members of the Dominican order are again represented. Some paintings were lost when sepulchral stones were set in the walls, others were destroyed in the bombings of 1943 which particularly damaged the Grazie group of buildings, almost completely destroying the Refectory, a considerable part of the left aisle chapels, the Cloister of the Dead and the Library. Today, five figures remain in the left aisle (Saint Peter Martyr, Blessed James de' Ariboldis of Monza, Blessed Reboald of Albenga, Saint Dominic, Blessed Reginald of Orleans) and five in the right aisle (unidentified saint holding a crucifix; Blessed Antonio Pavoni of Savigliano; another unidentified saint in adoration before an image of the Virgin; a saint indicated in the inscription, which is not original, as Blessed Antonio d'As; a martyred saint of whom only the bust remains).

These frescoes must logically have been painted immediately after the building was finished (1482), and their approximate chronology (1482–85 ca.), also fits in with the history of their probable author, Bernardino Butinone, whose name was first mentioned by Gattico and confirmed by Mongeri and successive historians.[2]

The tondos of the nave were freed from the seventeenth century overpainting only in 1892, by Luca Beltrami, and then during the through 1935–37 restorations. Their attribution is not settled, but it seems likely that they were done by a team of painters supervised by Butinone and including Zenale and Montorfano.[3]

While Zenale's presence is difficult to identify exactly, Butinone's work stands out clearly (the busts of Saint Peter Martyr and Saint Thomas are stylistically very similar to the figures of Dominican saints on the pilasters) as does Montorfano's (see particularly his Saint Catherine of Siena and Saint Dominic) which can be compared with his paintings in the Refectory.

I believe that the same team of artists, in the same period also painted the lost decorations of the Cloister of the Dead and the Chapter Hall. Gattico suggested Montorfano as their author, which seems more likely than de' Rossi, whose name was put forward by Salmi after Santambrogio, for no solid reason, had attributed the original decoration of the Refectory to him.[4]

Another group of painters, working around the same time as the team we have just considered, must have created an

*Bernardino Butinone and
assistants (probably Donato
Montorfano), Saint Sebastian,
foreshortened tondo in the nave*

important work which today is unfortunately not easy to appreciate because it has been moved from its original site. Considering the building history of the Grazie group and the stylistic evidence, it should probably be dated slightly earlier than the other. This is the fresco that decorated the arch above the altar in the Lady Chapel.

After being covered by the seventeenth century stuccoes, it was brought to light after the 1943 bombing. The painting depicts *The Eternal Surrounded by Angels* and was probably done by Bonifacio Bembo's workshop. The most obvious comparison is with the decoration in the Ducal Chapel of the Castello Sforzesco, done by Bembo and his assistants around 1472–73.[5] The comparison justifies dating it to a period before the church was completed, setting it back to a moment in Milanese painting immediately preceding the success of Butinone, Zenale and Montorfano, and the first steps of Leonardo, Bramante and the young Bramantino.

Quattrocentesque Work in the Chapels and Refectory
The prestige of the new Dominican church, confirmed by the attention that the Milanese ducal family gave to it from its foundation, must early have induced a number of important personalities to reserve a burial place there. The present situation of the chapels and the many funeral monuments is the result of transformations over the centuries produced in part by the same causes which have modified almost all the great monasterial groups over time. Some evidence remains of the first fifteenth century contributions by private citizens of Milan. The earliest is the funeral monument of the Della Torre family, placed in the first chapel on the right in 1935–37 and originally in the Lady Chapel. It was commissioned by Francesco Della Torre in 1483, as the tablet set below the urn recalls. The tomb, supported by two candelabrum columns, is composed of a rectangular urn ornamented on the front by three reliefs (*Annunciation, Adoration of the Shepherds, Adoration of the Magi*) and on the sides by two coats of arms. The cover, on which is represented the bust of the Eternal Father, is crowned by a *genietto*.

The structure of the monument is closely related to Lombard sculpture of the second part of the Quattrocento and in the past was attributed to Amadeo. Now it is thought to be the work of the brothers Tomaso and Francesco Cazzaniga, since it is very similar to the Brivio monument in the church of Sant'Eustorgio, begun by Francesco Cazzaniga and entrusted after his death to Tomaso Cazzaniga and Benedetto Briosco.[6]

Another surviving Quattrocento contribution due to a pri-

Bonifacio Bembo's workshop, The Eternal Surrounded by Angels, decoration of the vault in the Lady Chapel

vate commission is to be seen in the fragmentary frescoes of the Bolla Chapel (first on the left side). Doubly fragmentary: because the cycle of paintings, dating from the last decade of the century, remained incomplete, and because the 1943 bombings almost completely destroyed two of the three frescoed lunettes.[7] The cycle was meant to illustrate the stories of Saint Catherine of Alexandria and Saint Catherine of Siena, but work was limited to the upper zone of the three walls. Today two episodes of Saint Catherine of Alexandria remain on the left wall (*Saint Catherine before the Emperor* and the *Argument of Saint Catherine with the Pagan Scholars*) and one only of the two episodes of Saint Catherine of Siena painted on the opposite wall (*Saint Catherine Received by the Pope*). Discovered only in 1928 and published by Salmi, the frescoes are of notable stylistic and compositive quality and have been attributed to Montorfano.[8]

This attribution seems doubtful, however, because in the works definitely known to be his, Montorfano never displays such accuracy of perspective and composition as we see here. These qualities on the other hand were typical of

87

Cristoforo de' Mottis (?),
Saint Catherine of Alexandria
before the Emperor,
Bolla Chapel, left wall

Cristoforo de' Mottis (?),
Argument of Saint Catherine
of Alexandria with the Pagan
Scholars, Bolla Chapel, left wall

Cristoforo de' Mottis, an interesting artist of the late Lombard Quattrocento who created the decoration of Saint Catherine's Chapel in the Sanctuary of Brea and cartoons for the windows of Saint John the Evangelist in Milan cathedral.

At this point we must consider Montorfano's work in the Grazie building. Besides the well known *Crucifixion*, recent research tends to attribute to him the whole decoration of the Refectory.[9] Today, after the 1943 destruction, only the painting along the left wall remains, but it shows close similarities with the decoration in the aisles of the church. For stylistic and technical reasons it is doubtful whether there was any lapse of time between this work and the vast *Crucifixion*, signed and dated 1495, so it is probable that the decoration should in fact be attributed to him and the unsupported hypothesis concerning Bernardino de' Rossi should be dropped once and for all.

As for the *Crucifixion*, one can only confirm the unenthusiastic evaluations of the critics who have made the obligatory comparison between this painting and Leonardo's masterpiece opposite, from which it has derived a fame it would hardly have deserved on its own merits. In the few other works which can justifiably be attributed to Montorfano (the frescoes now in the Ambrosiana, from Santa Maria della Rosa, and those of Saint Anthony's Chapel in the church of San Pietro in Gessate) the style is very similar and the artist remains within formulas typical of Paduan painting. His limits are more evident in this large composition in which different elements are brought together without any real spatial unity or narrative tension. To mention Bramante in this context is meaningless, even as an inspiration for the fantastic view of Jerusalem which appears in the background. Lacking a real perspectival firmness, the construction fails to create the unified space that a more skilful use of the motif would have given. Montorfano's *Crucifixion* brings us to the "Bramantesque" period of the Grazie, which will be examined in detail in the following paragraph. Culturally, however, it belongs to the preceding period, as does the votive fresco today placed in the first chapel of the right aisle, where it was mooved from the Lady Chapel immediately after the war. It portrays the *Madonna in Adoration before the Child with Two Saints and the Donor and His Family*, and is interesting chiefly as a votive painting. This makes it difficult to place: some aspects in fact would date it to halfway through the century, while others already show the influence of Leonardo. At all events, the section with the portraits of the patron and his family is charming and also important as a document.[10]

Late fifteenth century Lombard painter, Madonna in Adoration before the Child with Two Saints and the Donor and His Family, first chapel of the right aisle

91

Around Bramante

Bramante's intervention in the Grazie marked a turning point, not only for the architecture but also for the decorations. This occurred not so much because of work directly done by the master, but because of the change in taste which ultimately can be traced back to his activity in Lombardy. The Bramantesque environment is clear in the interior and exterior decorations of the apse, although it is difficult to establish to what extent, if at all, the work is based on his design. If we consider the exterior, the decorated part on the upper sections of the apses (candelabra alternating with parastades and medallions containing profiles of saints) appears very elegant but can hardly be connected to Bramante because the evidence of the Lombard tradition is so strong (similarities with the façade of the Certosa of Pavia and the Colleoni Chapel at Bergamo). However, it should be noted that it has the same module as decoration which runs round the drum of the dome, although in the latter the ornamental effect is obtained exclusively through an elegant chromatic contrast, the elements which compose it being reduced to stylized forms. Inside the Bramantesque apse, further puzzling questions are raised by the graffito decoration which covers the walls almost entirely. Restoration work which has just been finished [11] has uncovered the surface of the dome, and the original chromatic values to the whole interior. In the light of what has already been discovered, it appears probable that Bramante's design included a graffito decoration of the plastered areas to give them vibrancy, using the slight difference of colour between the final coat of *intonaco* and the one underneath to create a barely perceptible chiaroscuro contrast.[12]

It is difficult to identify any specific references for the whole graffito decoration, obviously executed by craftsmen. However, it has been rightly pointed out that at least the most important part (the four tondos in the spandrels of the cupola, depicting the Doctors of the Church) can be connected to Bramante's circle, and more specifically to Bramantino.[13]

The presence of the latter, the most outstanding artist of the early Milanese Cinquecento, can be identified more or less directly in the decorations of the Bramantesque areas (apse, small cloister and Old Sacristy). The lunette over the entrance portal to the Old Sacristy, with a monochrome representation of the *Madonna and Child between Saint Louis and Saint James*, has been justifiably attributed to him.[14] The presence of Saint Louis indicates that the painting was done during the period of French domination in Milan at the beginning of the sixteenth century.

*Lombard painter, Resurrection of
the Son of the Widow of Nain,
1520 ca., Old Sacristy, left-hand
panel of a cupboard*

Anonymous, Madonna and Child with Saints Jerome, Dominic, Peter the Martyr and Nicholas of Bari, with the Patron Nicolò Lachesnave, 1517, fresco in the apse

Before we go on to other Cinquecento works, a monument should be mentioned which is no longer preserved in the Grazie but which was commissioned by Ludovico il Moro as one of the most important elements of his plan to make the Bramantesque apse into a mausoleum for himself and his family. The project was interrupted by the well known political events and of the tomb carved by Cristoforo Solari (for which the artist was given marble in 1494 and 1497) only the cover remains, portraying the recumbent figures of Ludovico il Moro and his wife Beatrice d'Este. After various events the cover was moved to the Certosa of Pavia, where it can still be seen today in the left transept of the church.[15]

French domination did not halt the work of completing and decorating the Grazie buildings. At least two important undertakings date from that period: the decoration of the Old Sacristy and the remodelling (and extension) of the wooden choir to fit the new apse of the church. The adaptation evidently required considerable new work,[16] as we can still see if we examine it today. The dossals of the lower order show typical Quattrocento intarsio decorations (geometrical designs created by juxtaposing different woods, without any overlaid colourings), while those of the

*Marco d'Oggiono, Saint John
the Baptist and a Knight of Malta,
seventh right-hand chapel, altar*

upper section (decorated with floral motives alternating with figures of saints) are done with a technique of carving and stucco indicating a later date. This would confirm the information and dates given by Gattico.[17]

Gattico's information appears less reliable concerning the cupboards of the Old Sacristy, made to hold the precious furnishings donated to the monastery by Ludovico il Moro after the death of Beatrice in 1497. He states that the cupboards on the left wall were finished in 1498 and those on the opposite wall were started in 1503. The first date given by Gattico probably refers to the beginning of the work, which seems to have been finished several years later according to a different design.

In fact only the pilasters and the first two doors of the left-hand cupboards are decorated with real intarsio, while all the rest is ornamented with paintings vaguely suggesting the same technique. This seems to indicate that the work was done in a period of economic difficulty, after the fall of Ludovico il Moro, but the style of the design suggests a much later date, in the second decade of the sixteenth century.[18] The scenes ornamenting the dossals above the cupboard illustrate fourteen episodes from the New Testament (left) and twenty-one from the Old Testament (right).

Although there are no particular reasons to suppose that the dossals of the two sides were done at different dates, there is a clear stylistic difference between them. While the New Testament scenes are definitely connected with Bramantino's painting, those from the Old Testament, which are much more summary and folk-like, seem linked, although less clearly, to the style of Gaudenzio Ferrari. The reference to Gaudenzio is not inappropriate, since at least two works testify to his presence in the monastery, as we shall see.

With the elegant decoration in the vault of the Old Sacristy, re-echoing the knot motif created by Leonardo for the Sala delle Asse in the Sforza Castle, the work of decoration was done in the presbytery and the apse, and in the first half of the nineteenth century the whole tribune, including the dome, was painted.[19]

Sixteenth and Seventeenth Centuries

The most important decoration of the sixteenth century was certainly that of the Chapel of the Holy Crown (the forty in the right aisle). The confraternity of Santa Corona, founded in 1494 with the aim of assisting the impoverished sick, from 1502 onwards had its own chapel in the Grazie church, named after a relic of the cross of thorns preserved there. The rectors of the confraternity were buried in the chapel. In 1539 the councillor Bernardino

*Gaudenzio Ferrari, fresco
decoration, vault of the
Chapel of the Holy Crown,
fourth left-hand chapel*

Ghilio left a will ordering an altarpiece to be painted for the chapel and scenes of the Passion to be represented on the walls. The altarpiece was commissioned from Titian, the frescoes from Gaudenzio Ferrari; both works were finished before the end of 1542.[20] Titian's great painting, the famous *Crown of Thorns*, was requisitioned by the French in 1797 and is now in the Louvre.[21] The style expressed by Titian in this painting, monumental and Mannerist in its tendency, can be found to some extent also in Gaudenzio's frescoes, although the latter does not completely abandon the narrative, dramatic vein typical of his first period.

Gaudenzio had moved to Milan around 1537 (he was to die there in 1546) and this is his earliest extant Milanese work. Art historians have in the main formulated a qualified judgement on it, even seeing it as mostly done by Giovan Battista della Cerva, who worked with Gaudenzio in Milan.

The frescoes cover the walls and vault: on the left wall there is a *Crucifixion*, on the right *Ecce Homo*, and below the *Flagellation*; while the vault cells display eight *Angels with the Instruments of the Passion*. These frescoes represent a Mannerist turn in Gaudenzio's work, influenced by Titian's altarpiece and the Milanese environment. This becomes clear when we compare them with an immediately preceding work done by the same painter in Santa Maria delle Grazie (Giulio Bora has drawn attention to this, recalling an old attribution which had been forgotten).[22] This is a fresco painted on the back wall of the Old Sacristy, representing two angels pulling back a curtain and below, an inscription tablet flanked by two cherubs. The tablet, placed by the governor of Milan, Alfonso d'Avalos, bears the name of Luigi de la Cueva and the date 1541. The original design of the composition is not clear because the space between the two angels has been occupied by a later, weak hand which has portrayed there a Dominican saint in prayer with a kneeling woman and child behind him. I think there is no doubt that the original part must be attributed to Gaudenzio and that here he appears much closer to his earlier style.

Finally, another work painted by Gaudenzio for the Grazie church was requisitioned by the French, like Titian's altarpiece. This is the Saint *Paul*, signed and dated 1543, now in the Musée des Beaux-Art at Lyons.[23] This painting fully confirms the Mannerist turn in Gaudenzio's style announced by the frescoes in the Chapel of the Holy Crown. There is an example of a more openly Mannerist style in another important decorative cycle completed in the same period: the frescoes and altarpiece of Saint Dominic's Chapel (the fifth in the left aisle) commissioned by

Lombard artist, Two Prophets flanking a panel depicting The Sending of the Archangel Gabriel to earth, third right-hand chapel, lunette on the right wall

Domenico Sauli who had obtained the patronage of the chapel in 1541. The altarpiece is dedicated to the *Cruci-fixion*, the frescoes in the vault to *Prophets and Sibyls*, those on the side walls to the *Journey to Emmaus* (left) and *Noli Me Tangere* (right).[24] The frescoes and the altarpiece were painted by Giovanni Demìo, but if his signature had not been discovered in 1936 the work would have remained without any attribution, so varied are its stylistic elements, reflecting the wide range of experiences of this Veneto artist. The influences he displays embrace most of the painting of North and Central Italy and also include Northern elements.[25]

Another "foreign" painter present in the Grazie in the second half of the century was the Genoese Ottavio Semino, who in the eighties painted in the Chapel of Saint John the Baptist (the last in the right aisle). Elegant stucco frames divide the vault into eight sections in which *Prophets* are represent, while on the walls there is a *Preaching of the Baptist* (left) and a *Decollation of Saint John* (right).[26] The rich stucco decorations and Semino's style, influenced by

*Coriolano Malagavazzo, Madonna
and Child between Saint Dominic
and Saint Laurence, 1595, Chapel
of Saint Vincent Ferreri, altar*

Cerano (Giovan Battista Crespi) and assistants, the Virgin Freeding Milan from the Plague, left aisle, last span

late Central Italy. Mannerism, make this chapel a noteworthy example of late Cinquecento taste.

The same taste appears in the decoration of the Marliani Chapel (third in the right aisle, dedicated to the Angels). The artist, who has not been definitely identified, painted *Angelic Choirs* in the vault and two couples of *Prophets* on the walls, flanking panels representing *Saint Michael Defeating Satan* (left) and the *Sending of the Archangel Gabriel to Earth* (right). The altarpiece, by the same hand depicts the *Incoronation of the Virgin with Saint Michael and Saint Jerome*.[27]

The same artistic tradition, enriched by knowledge of the great painters of the early Lombard Seicento, appears in the frescoes of the Chapel of Saint Vincent Ferreri (sixth in the right aisle). These are the work of the brothers Giovan Battista and Giovan Mauro della Rovere, called "I Fiammenghini." On the left wall there are two *Episodes from the Life of Saint Vincent Ferreri* and on the right, two scenes of the *Martyrdom of Saint Vincent Deacon*. The instruments of torture referring to the martyrdom are displayed by four angels painted in the vault. A greater narrative clarity and a decided emphasis on the macabre show that we are now in a fully developed Seicento climate, while the altarpiece suggests the final phase of Lombard Mannerism. Dedicated to the *Madonna with Child between Saint Dominic and Saint Laurence*, it is dated 1595 and signed by Coriolano Malagavazzo, a pupil of Bernardino Campi.

The artistic culture of the Seicento, which had a period of marked expansion in Milan mainly thanks to the initiatives promoted by Federico Borromeo, left notable traces in the Grazie which unfortunately, however, have only partly survived. As an expression of the city's gratitude for the ending of the plague in 1630, Cerano was commissioned to paint a great lunette to be placed above the entrance to the Lady Chapel, at the end of the left aisle. Although the work was probably done chiefly by assistants (Melchiorre Gherardini in particular), the lunette with *The Virgin Freeing Milan from the Plague* testifies to Cerano's sensitivity and his ability to render the climate of gloomy desolation created by the plague.[28]

In the same period the Lady Chapel was completely remodelled and decorated throughout with a rich fresco and stucco ornamentation, destroyed by the 1943 bombings. Melchiorre Gherardini's frescoes on the wall outside the chapel were lost, but his great stucco lunette, representing the *Madonna of the Rosary Surrounded by Saints and Devotees*, remains, covering the whole left wall of the central nave outside the chapel. Recently restored,[29] the lunette appears of notable quality. Based on the contrast between white figures and a sky-blue background, the composition seems to be imitating a Della Robbia relief, with very elegant results, while the definition of the faces and drapery has a dignity that goes beyond mere craftsmanship.

Of the other surviving seventeenth-century contributions, the frescoes by Stefano Danedi in the apse of the Old Sacristy should be mentioned,[30] together with the altarpiece by the same artists depicting the *Madonna and Child Appearing to Saint Rose of Lima*, now in the sixth chapel of the left aisle.[31]

From the Eighteenth Century to the Present Day

The "new" decoration of the presbytery and apse dated from the first decades of the eighteenth century; this was completely removed in 1935–37, together with the decoration of the tribune done in the first half of the nineteenth century. The restoration of 1935–37, although performed according to criteria which today are largely unacceptable, marks an important date in the history of the Grazie, as does the destruction caused by the 1943 bombings.

With these events it can be said that the historical development of Santa Maria delle Grazie came to an end. Obviously its life did not stop, and there were further restorations and new acquisitions.

Among the latter, the following should be mentioned: in the first chapel of the left aisle (already mentioned as the Bolla Chapel), above the altar six bronze low reliefs representing *Episodes of Saint Catherine of Siena* have been placed as a gift from the artist Francesco Messina (1981); in the fourth chapel on the left there are the tombs of Senator Ettore Conti (patron of the 1935–37 restorations) and his wife, by Federico Wildt (1935). Above the altar in the same chapel there is a triptych, *Madonna and Child between Saints John the Baptist and Peter Martyr*, signed and dated Niccolò da Cremona 1520 (a painter otherwise unknown), in deposit from the Brera gallery.

On the left wall of the fifth chapel in the left aisle there is a painting by Paris Bordon, *Holy Family with Saint Catherine of Alexandria*, in deposit from the Certosa of Pavia. On the right wall of the same chapel hangs a canvas recently donated to the Grazie portraying the *Miracle of Saint Ludovic Bertrán*, identified with a painting by Giambattista Lucini for the church of San Domenico at Crema.[32] In the second chapel of the right aisle, the altarpiece portraying *Saint Martin de Porres in Ecstasy before the Cross* is by Silvio Consadori (1962).

[1] The identification of these figures and those portrayed in the niches of pilasters in the side aisles is given by A.M. Caccin O.P., *Santa Maria delle Grazie e il Cenacolo Vinciano*, Milan 1985 (4th ed.) pp. 54–55.

[2] P.G. Gattico O.P., *Descrizione succinta e vera delle cose spettanti alla Chiesa e Convento di Santa Maria delle Grazie e di Santa Maria della Rosa e suo luogo e altre loro aderenze in Milano dell'Ordine dei Predicatori*, ms. (eighteenth century). Archivio di Stato di Milano, Fondo di Religione, p.a., Conventi, Milan, cart. 1398; G. Mongeri, *L'arte in Milano*, Milan 1872, p. 214; M. Salmi, "Bernardino Butinone," in *Dedalo*, 10,1929-30, p. 341; F. Mazzini, *Affreschi lombardi del Quattrocento*, Milan 1965, p. 474; G. Mulazzani, "La decorazione pittorica: il Quattrocento" in *Santa Maria delle Grazie in Milano*, Milan 1983, p. 115.

[3] F. Mazzini, *op. cit.*, p. 474.

[4] M. Salmi, *Il Cenacolo di Leonardo da Vinci e la Chiesa delle Grazie a Milano*, Milan, n.d. (but 1926), comment on plate 11; D. Santambrogio, "Bernardino de' Rossi in Santa Maria delle Grazie in Milano," in *Archivio Storico dell'arte*, 1, 1895, pp. 20–32.

[5] G. Mulazzani, *op. cit.*, p. 117; the attribution to Bembo is by Gengaro ("Breve percorso tra gli anonimi lombardi del Quattrocento," in *Arte Lombarda*, 3, 1958, pp. 75–79), whereas Mazzini (*op. cit.*, pp. 480–81) suggests early Montorfano.

[6] On this bomb and the main sculptural work in the Grazie, see L. Giordano's essay "La scultura," in *Santa Maria delle Grazie...*, cit., pp. 90–110. Of the other funeral monuments, all smaller in size, the most important is that of Branda Castiglioni (a slab with relief labels, surmounted by a lunette containing the portrait of the deceased, who died in 1495), placed in the second chapel of the left aisle. Four sixteenth century cenotaphs once in the aisle were transferred during the 1935–37 restorations to the second chapel in the right aisle.

[7] The approximate dating of the frescoes is based on the fact that in 1490 the patron, the jurisconsult Francesco Bolla, died; on the other hand it may be supposed that the cause of the interruption of the work was related to the fall of Ludovico il Moro. On the frescoes and their attribution to Cristoforo de' Mottis, cf. G. Mulazzani, *op. cit.*, pp. 119–22.

[8] M. Salmi, "Gli affreschi scoperti in Santa Maria delle Grazie a Milano," in *Bollettino d'Arte*, s. II, 8, 1928, pp. 3–13; the attribution to Montorfano is taken up again by Mazzini, "Problemi pittorici bramanteschi," in *Bollettino d'Arte*, s. IV, 49, 1964, p. 340.

[9] Cf. G. Martelli, "Il Refettorio di Santa Maria delle Grazie in Milano e il restauro di Luca Beltrami nell'ultimo decennio dell'Ottocento," in *Bollettino d'Arte*, 8, 1980, pp. 55–72. On Montorfano and the relative bibliography, cf. G. Mulazzani, *op. cit.*, pp. 122–30.

[10] Salmi (*Il "Cenacolo...."* cit., comment on plate 38) notes that the woman and little girl are dressed in Spanish style, following a fashion introduced by Isabella of Aragon who married Gian Galeazzo in 1489. For other observations, cf. F. Mazzini, *Affreschi...*, cit., p. 485.

[11] The restoration has revealed the graffiti of the cupola, uncovering the original plaster which is almost completely preserved. During the 1935–37 restoration, perhaps with the aim of matching the colour of the calotte to the rest of the tribune (cf. A. Pica, P. Portaluppi, *Le Grazie*, Rome 1938, pp. 166–67), after the neoclassical decoration was removed the whole surface was recoloured and the graffiti, concealed again, were picked out by brush. The restoration, financed by the Ministero per i Beni Culturali e Ambientali, has been executed by Giovanni Rossi, under the supervision of Germano Mulazzani.

[12] Pica and Portaluppi (*op. cit.*, p. 167) correctly distinguish three groups of graffiti: in the pendentives, in the dome and in the presbytery.

[13] G. Bora, "La decorazione pittorica: sino al Settecento," in *Santa Maria delle Grazie....* cit., pp. 140–43.

[14] Cf. G. Mulazzani, *L'opera completa del Bramantino e Bramante pittore*, Milan 1978, p. 92. The other lunette preserved in the same cloister, above the door to the church, with two Dominican saints painted in monochrome flanking a low relief portraying the Madonna and Child, can be as-

cribed generically to Bramantino's workshop. A similar opinion must be expressed about the fragment of fresco showing the Nativity, transferred from the Lady Chapel and preserved inside the monastery; cf. G. Mulazzani, *op. cit.*, p. 132.

[15] On Cristoforo Solari (called "Il Gobbo") as a sculptor, cf. G. Nicodemi, in *Storia di Milano*, X, Milan 1957, pp. 791-94.

[16] On the history and characteristics of the choir, see B. Ciati, "Il coro," in *Santa Maria delle Grazie...*, cit., pp. 214-23.

[17] Ciati (*op. cit.*, p. 219) appropriately compares the tarsie of the upper stalls to those of the choir of the Abbey of Viboldone, signed by Francesco Giramo di Abbiategrasso and dated 1522.

[18] I set out this idea in the essay already cited (G. Mulazzani, *op. cit.*, pp. 132-33).

[19] All the eighteenth- and nineteenth-century decorations were removed during the restoration promoted by senator Ettore Conti, the results of which were described in the monograph by A. Pica, P. Portaluppi, *op. cit.* On this intervention, Luca Beltrami's restoration and the work following the 1943 bombing, cf. L. Gremmo, "I restauri," in *Santa Maria delle Grazie...*, cit., pp. 196-213.

[20] On the Holy Crown Chapel cf. G. Bora, *op. cit.*, pp. 152-61. The relative documents were published by P. Cannetta, *Storia del Pio Istituto di Santa Corona di Milano*, Milan 1883.

[21] On the importance of this painting in the work of Titian, cf. R. Pallucchini, *Tiziano*, Florence 1969, I, p. 93. For the painter's connections with Milan and a review of the Milanese artists' environment of this period, see the essays by G. Bora and P. De Vecchi in *Omaggio a Tiziano*, Milan 1977, pp. 45-54 and 55-86.

[22] G. Bora, *La decorazione...*, cit., pp. 157-58. The attribution had been suggested, and not taken up again later, by D. Santambrogio, "L'iscrizione Davalos nella Sagrestia leonardesca di S.M. delle Grazie e due putti ascrivibili a Gaudenzio," in *Osservatore Cattolico*, 8 August 1908.

[23] On the exact placing of the altarpiece in the first chapel on the right, dedicated to Saint Paul, cf. G. Bora, *La decorazione...*, cit., pp. 160-61.

[24] On the strange stucco decoration which occupies the lower part of the side walls, portraying *Angels with the Instruments of the Passion*, I agree with Luisa Giordano (*op. cit.*, pp. 161-64) who considers it the work of a skilful nineteenth-century imitator.

[25] On Demio, see V. Sgarbi, in *Da Tiziano a El Greco*, exhibition catalogue, Milan 1981, pp. 123-24. Bora proposes a date around 1541, the year in which Domenico Sauli obtained the patronage of the chapel, which seems to me correct (*La decorazione...*, cit., pp. 161-64).

[26] The altarpiece of the chapel, representing *Saint John the Baptist and a Devotee*, is by Marco d'Oggiono and was moved here, together with the al-

tar, from the Old Sacristy.

[27] Torre (*Il Ritratto di Milano*, Milan 1714, p. 151) attributes the frescoes and the altarpiece to Semino, while Pica ("Restauro della Cappella Marliani in Santa Maria delle Grazie a Milano," in *Arti*, 7, 1975, pp. 31-36) assigns them to Aurelio and G. Pietro Luini, Bora (*La decorazione...*, cit., p. 170) dates the decorations to the first decade of the seventeenth century, and rather cautiously suggests Francesco Nappi as their author.

[28] On this work by Cerano, cf. G. Bora, *La decorazione...*, cit., pp. 175-76, and M. Rosci, *Mostra del Cerano*, Novara 1964, pp. 118-19.

[29] The restoration, privately financed, was done by Claudio Fociani (1985).

[30] The correct attribution was taken up by Giulio Bora (*La decorazione...*, cit., p. 178) after it had been published by Caselli (*Nuovo ritratto di Milano in riguardo alle belle arti*, Milan 1827), and subsequently forgotten.

[31] This chapel belonged in the past to the Borromeo family and an alteration is documented, promoted by Saint Charles Borromeo who wished to bury his parents there. The work was entrusted to Pellegrino Tibaldi in 1575. The traces of Tibaldi's intervention were cancelled by the restoration of 1935-37. Tibaldi's design has been found by Bora in the Archivio Vescovile of Milan: G. Bora, *La decorazione...*, cit., p. 164.

[32] The identification of the painting, which is by Cesare Alpini, is given by G. Bora, *La decorazione...*, cit., p. 180.

Photo credits
Archivio Electa, Milano
Archivio Motta, Milano
Antonio Quattrone, Firenze
© The Royal Collection,
Her Majesty Queen Elisabeth II,
Windsor

This book was printed by Elemond S.p.A.
at the plant in Martellago (Venice) in 1999